Rip Off!

8-2-13

To Paul
SAFE trip BACk
Enjoyed your company
David

Other books by Paul Taylor

Ripping Yarns
Ripping Yarns 2
Why We Are Australian
Awesome Aussies

RIP OFF!

Australian Fraud,
Deception and Dirty Tricks

Paul Taylor

The Five Mile Press

The Five Mile Press Pty Ltd
1 Centre Road, Scoresby
Victoria 3179 Australia
www.fivemile.com.au

Copyright © Paul Taylor, 2011
All rights reserved

First published 2011

Printed in Australia

Cover design by Debra Billson
Page design by Shaun Jury
Cover images: Daisy Bates, 'Breaker' Morant, Ned Kelly and Shane Warne © Newspix; Al Grassby by Michael Jones © Newspix, Alan Bond by Ian Munro © Newspix; TE Lawrence courtesy Imperial War Museum

National Library of Australia Cataloguing-in-Publication entry
    Taylor, Paul
    Rip Off!: Australian fraud, deception and dirty tricks / Paul Taylor.
    ISBN: 9781742481272 (pbk.)
    Fraud – Australia.
    364.163

Contents

Preface ... 1

THE SCAMS
Obtaining money by means of deception

Sudden Solomon's Grate Bank Robbery ... 7
The Kangaroo Gang and Arthur Delaney ... 11
The Great Bookie Robbery and the Wolf Pack's End ... 17

THE FRAUDS
Intentional misrepresentation or concealment of information in order to deceive or mislead

Field Marshal Blamey's Inglorious Life ... 25
Alan Bond and the Lost Billions ... 35
The *Trial* and the Treachery ... 39
The Dirty Double Dealings of Al Grassby ... 45
Marcus Einfeld: The Hubris of a Living Legend ... 53
Captain Moonlite's Walk on the Wild Side ... 59
The Truth about Wilfred Burchett ... 67
When Daisy Bates Met the Breaker ... 73
Storm's Scandal and Carlton's Blue ... 83
Peter Foster and The Riddle of His Underpants Escape ... 89

THE HOAXES
Something that has been established or accepted by fraudulent means

The Imagination of Frank Hardy ... 97

Ern Malley Turns on His Frankensteins	103
TE Lawrence and the Ambush of the Light Horse	109
Awful Arthur Orton, the Man Who Hoodwinked Two Nations	115

THE STINGS
A confidence game planned and executed with care

The Sport of Kings – and Knaves	129
Fine Cotton and the Sting in the Horse's Tale	135

THE DECEPTIONS
A ruse; a trick

How Horrie the Wog Dog Fooled Us All	145
Francis de Groot and The Day He Saw Red	151
Murdoch's Wapping War	157
Gallipoli and the Triumphant Retreat	163
The Governor-General's Surprise	171
Shane Warne. Now You See It, Now You Don't	183
Len Lawson. A Monster Behind the Mask	187

THE RIPPED OFF
Exploitation, esp. of those who cannot prevent or counter it.

Rupert Murdoch and the Man He Saved	193
Ned Kelly's Case. Still Not Closed	199
Azaria Chamberlain	217
Gun Alley and the Man Fit to be Hanged	221

THE DEBATABLE
Having strong points on both sides that can be questioned or disputed

Men at Work and the Down Under Plunder	229
Jim and Juni and the Love that – Finally – Spoke Its Name	233
AGW and the History Wars. As One Cools, the Other Heats Up	241

Preface

They laughed when I sat down to write this book. 'What are you calling it?' they'd ask. '**RIP OFF!**' I'd tell them. 'A panorama of Australian fraud, deception and dirty tricks over the centuries.'

Two beats later they'd ask another question to which they knew the answer: '*Do* we have rip offs in Australia?'

That always got a big laugh.

Well, I thought, I've stumbled upon something here. A book whose title alone sends people into paroxysms of hilarity. Bestseller list here I come!

The truth, however, is that the laughter was bitter. Cynical. Sad. Because the stories of Australian rip offs go back centuries: an age-old tale of corrupt politicians, bent judges, police commissioners on the payroll of criminals, share market manipulators and paper shufflers, high-fliers like Christopher Skase, and VIP tax cheats.

But theirs are not necessarily enthralling stories. Essentially they are accounts of greed and not much more. Of course the rip-off merchants, such as Edward G Robinson's character Johnny Rocco, in *Key Largo*, are not satisfied with money earned honestly. And they are not satisfied with what they've got illegally. They want more. 'That's right, I want more!' Rocco says in a flash of self-revelation.

But *Key Largo,* aside from Robinson's egregious character, also had Humphrey Bogart, Lauren Bacall, Lionel Barrymore, steamy sex and smoking guns. Now *that's* a story. Christopher Skase had Pixie, emphysema, and exile on a rundown villa on an arid, dusty landscape in Spain. That's a story, but it's not particularly absorbing. Abe Goldberg, who fled Australia with $1.5 billion missing from his rag-trade business and was found 15 years later in Poland is of interest to those he owes money, but otherwise he's just another businessman from the Golden Rip-Off Age, the 1980s, when banks fell over themselves to shovel millions at people like him.

The stories in this book, I believe, could all be made into movies. They begin in the early 19th century with the Grate Bank Robbery. They end with the heat going out of the climate change debate and the still simmering Australian history wars. Both would make gripping feature films: Sudden Solomon and his convict crew burrowing their way into the bank in old Sydney Town. A classic caper movie. And the climate change blockbuster: the dramatic account of a bubble pricked by leaked emails followed almost immediately by once alarmist world leaders tiptoeing from Copenhagen and hoping that AGW would, just as quietly, go away. I see it as an enthralling cliffhanger with, perhaps, Danny De Vito in a wig and cast against type as Kevin Rudd, and Denzel Washington playing President Obama. And the history wars. An explosive battle ignited by the research of one man, a Left apostate, infuriatingly finding gross errors in academic shibboleths. An intellectual, provocative movie with Rusty Crowe as the lone warrrior.

At the heart of almost all the stories in this book, is deceit, but not all of it malevolent. Rupert Murdoch, for instance, makes two appearances – in both he emerges a hero, a lifesaver. Murdoch saved a man from the gallows (and how many of us can say that?); and his fight against the London print unions saved the world's most vibrant and exciting newspaper centre. The evacuation of Gallipoli, too, was based on trickery, but what a magnificent deception! Daisy Bates and Breaker Morant fabricated a past built on wishful thinking. And who could blame them? And the story of how Horrie the

Wog Dog was saved by the cunning of his owners – now *there's* a marvellous movie - is proof that there is more to a rip-off than the egregious Johnny Rocco's whine, 'I want more!'

Some of the stories here have appeared in other books of mine. I've included them because I believe they're classics of their type. Had I excluded them you may have felt ripped off.

Paul Taylor

THE SCAMS

Obtaining money
by means of deception

Sudden Solomon's GRATE BANK ROBBERY

How Sudden Solomon earned his nickname is not known, but it's likely that it had to do with quick wits in the service of wrongdoing. Sudden Solomon was a master safecracker.

Highly esteemed in the London underworld, he nevertheless found himself employed – the curse of the criminal class – as a blacksmith, the price of escaping the gallows in return for a free passage to Botany Bay. On an August morning in Sydney, 1828, now labouring under the less-spectacular name of William Blackston, he stumbled over a heaven-sent opportunity to go back to his sinful past. The heel of Blackston's boot jammed in a grate covering a large drain, all that was left of the Tank Stream, an old, almost-forgotten waterway in Lower George Street that had once been the convict settlement's major water supply.

As Blackston picked himself up – no doubt with a stout oath – he saw that the drain led to the foundations of the Bank of Australia: the path, he realised, to his early retirement.

Sudden Solomon – he was in Sudden Solomon mode now – knew what he had to do. The only question was who he was to do it with. He chose a shrewd old lag, Thomas Turner, who had worked on the building of the bank when it was founded only two years before. Turner was able to draw a plan of the bank, its strongroom and its drainage tunnels. He told Blackston that the mortar of the brickwork foundation was of a poor quality. He would not help dig – he feared his part in the robbery would be readily apparent – but he had earned, he argued, an equal share.

Blackston was up early a few weeks later taking measurements at four in the morning. At his forge he hammered crowbars, chisels and picks fashioned specifically for the break-in. With two trusted fellow ticket-of-leave men on board, Edward Farrell and Charles Dingle, Blackston felt they were ready. On the evening of Friday, 12 September 1828, they prised up the grate, entered the drain and, deep underground, began digging into the nine-feet-thick sandstone foundations. They made encouraging progress but on Saturday morning Blackston had to work at the forge, and when he finally joined Farrell and Dingle he found that they had recruited a fourth man, Clayton. Clayton, the others said, had laid the brick floor of the strongroom and his expertise could be helpful.

Sunday-morning church parade was compulsory for all convicts, but Dingle, with a little bribery and the old boys' convict network, had arranged exemption permits for his three fellow workers. They had been hard at it for some hours when to their fright, and then intense irritation, a fifth man loomed up from the blackness behind. They shone a lantern on him and he introduced himself: Val Rook. He had been sent by Dingle to tell Farrell, Clayton and Blackston that his exemption scheme had worked. It was thoughtful of Dingle, but entirely unnecessary, and now there were half a dozen in on the plan. No sooner was Val Rook in than a man named Woodward joined the party. Seven now, to share the spoils.

On Sunday afternoon, 13 September 1828, Sudden Solomon punched a crowbar through mortar and a brick tumbled down. He reached up into a hole. More bricks fell until there was a small square, enough, in a squeeze, for little Edward Farrell to be pushed through.

Australia's first bank robbery was about to take place. Farrell found himself standing, as Sudden Solomon had calculated, in the strongroom of the Bank of Australia. Sudden Solomon handed up a lantern and Farrell looked around. He was surrounded by padlocked strong boxes. In them was £14,500 in notes, £750 in British silver, 2000 gold sovereigns and 2309 Spanish dollars. Farrell broke the padlocks and began filling blue ticking bags for each man to carry away.

News of the burglary was greeted almost universally with hilarity and joy. Sydney had only two banks, the Bank of New South Wales, known as the People's Bank, and the Bank of Australia, known as the Gentlemen's Bank. Founded by John Macarthur and his ilk – wealthy squatters, merchants and landowners – the bank's loss had thousands of old lags drinking to the other, unknown old lags, who were now as wealthy as any of their Gentlemen betters.

Blackston spent his share very quickly, most likely in a gambling den in Macquarie Street. A year after he had come into his fortune and lost it he decided to try to get it back. He broke into the gambling house with an accomplice. A night watchman discovered them, fired a brace of pistols, and shot dead Blackston's crony and wounded Blackston in the shoulder. Blackston got life imprisonment on Norfolk Island.

The prospect of life on the island under Commandant Morisset, a sadist the convicts called King Lash, was too much for Blackston. He stood it for 18 months and then asked to speak to the Commandant. He could tell all about the robbery of the Bank of Australia, he said, in return for a full pardon.

In June 1831, Farrell, Dingle and Woodward stood trial. Clayton had drowned in the meantime, and Rook and Turner had long since disappeared. The three were sentenced to hang, but the sentence was later commuted to 10 years in the road gangs. Blackston joined them on the roads a short while later. He had been waiting for a ship to take him back to the Old Dart, his reward for shelfing his mates, when he was caught shoplifting. After his release, somewhat understandably, he took to the bottle. Sudden Solomon drank himself to death. In 1844, he stumbled, fell facedown in a Woolloomooloo swamp and didn't have the wit to get up. He was found that way the next day.

It was a last, fatal trip for Sudden Solomon.

The Kangaroo Gang and ARTHUR DELANEY

Miniskirts and marijuana; Mick and Keith and Marianne; Twiggy and the Shrimp; Pete and Dud; John, Paul, George and Ringo; the Maharishi; the Kings Road and kipper ties; Lord Astor, Christine Keeler and Mandy Rice-Davies; Albert Finney; Julie London; the Great Train Robbery, Ronnie Biggs and Slipper of the Yard; Nobby Stiles, Bobby Charlton and the World Cup; *The Avengers* and *Monty Python*.

'It was the best of times, it was the *best* of times,' Charles Dickens might have said had he been around at that best of times.

Ronnie Kray said something similar, but more crudely of course, in his autobiography, imaginatively titled *My Story*. 'They were the best years of our lives. They called them the swinging sixties. The Beatles and the Rolling Stones were rulers of pop music and me and my brother ruled London. We were fucking untouchable.'

Ronnie was exaggerating . . . a little, but it is true to say that for a large part of the sixties the Kray Twins, Ronnie and Reg and their gang – the Firm – were a notorious and integral part of the London cavalcade in the 1960s.

This horrible pair – Reg was a schizophrenic psychopath – and Ronnie was a sadist who had an affair with the deviant MP Lord

Boothby, inspired *Monty Python*'s celebrated Piranha Brothers. Dinsdale and Doug Piranha were twins born on probation and a week apart in London's East End. Although their gang – 'the Gang' – took over and terrorised London, you couldn't find anyone who had a bad word to say against them. 'Dinsdale, he was a nice boy . . . he nailed my head to the floor,' was a typical compliment.

The Piranha Brothers were an exaggeration, but their real life counterparts were celebrities who fascinated Fleet Street journalists as Melbourne and Sydney mobsters fascinate the Australian media today. They were on TV, they were photographed at their West End nightclubs with Frank Sinatra and Judy Garland, and when they were not posing for cameras they were plotting hold-ups, arson, protection rackets, horrific tortures and murders. At the Blind Beggar, an East End pub, Ronnie Kray strolled in one night and saw his gangland rival George Cornell sitting at the bar. George had called Ronnie 'a fat poof'. The jukebox was playing the Walker Brothers' hit 'The Sun Ain't Gonna Shine Anymore' and Ronnie shot George between the eyes 'The sun ain't gonna shine for him anymore,' said Ronnie.

The Krays were the royalty of gangland until Detective Superintendent Leonard 'Nipper' Reid – Nipper of the Yard not to be confused with Slipper of the Yard – finally caught up with them. But they were not alone. The Krays rivals, the Richardson brothers, the Great Train Robbers and the underworld connections that bubbled to the surface in the aftermath of the Christine Keeler–John Profumo scandal, all jostled for space on the front pages of the tabloids.

All this criminal and espionage activity meant that the police, 'the Old Bill', who didn't carry guns and were immortalised in Roger Miller's 'England Swings' lyrics: 'England swings like a pendulum do / Bobbies on bicycles two by two' were left plodding. They certainly weren't over-bothered about a bunch of Australians who were shoplifting.

In 1968 these shoplifters made it into the press. The international press. 'A giant shoplifting spree is plaguing Britain,' the *Los Angeles Times* reported. 'Foreigners carry a share of the blame, particularly a gang of Australian and New Zealand professionals who are driving Scotland Yard mad.'

'Driving Scotland Yard mad' was a large exaggeration. The shoplifters, jewel thieves inevitably dubbed the 'Kangaroo Gang', had been on a crime spree spread over the sixties in the UK and on the continent. Shoplifting on a huge scale, true. Over the decade the plunder amounted to hundreds of millions of pounds but it was done with such finesse and subtlety – no-one ever got hurt, there were no guns or coshes – that those famous Knightsbridge stores and Bond Street jewellers who were robbed were reluctant to advertise the fact; it might make upper-class customers uneasy, and give the lower class an incentive to try their luck. So the newspapers took little notice. The insurance companies paid up and when, once in a while, a Kangaroo Gang member was caught there were the options of bribing the Old Bill (not an uncommon practice), paying a fine or, at worst, ' porridge' for at most three years as a guest of Her Majesty.

That suited the police, occupied as they were with the more grisly side of the underworld. Detective Chief Superintendent Jack Slipper, Slipper of the Yard, was more interested in catching the Great Train Robber Ronnie Biggs, who was living in Melbourne at the time helping make sets for Channel Nine so that Graham Kennedy could knock them over on *In Melbourne Tonight*. And Nipper of the Yard was walking on the wilder side of London's East End, trying to find someone who might shop Reggie or Ronnie: 'Nah, they're diamond geezers. Kind to their Mum. I never saw nuffink, did I?'

So it was left to Detective Constable Jimmy 'Smudger' Smith of the Yard and the men of the new C11 Squad to bring the Kangaroo Gang to justice. Smudger had an advantage in that he was considered formidable enough to be given a nickname, but he was up against Australian crims with nicknames like Arthur 'the Duke' Delaney, Billy 'the General' Hill, Jack 'the Fibber' Warren and William 'Wee Jimmy' Lloyd. It was no contest.

The Duke, the General, the Fibber, and Wee Jimmy all headed collaborating gangs of thieves, mostly Australians who had found life in Sydney and Melbourne too hot and had come to the cooler climate of London where they had it all their way for half a dozen years.

Then in 1967, the Yard fessed up. There *was* a problem and it couldn't solve it. For the first time the *Police Gazette* listed dozens of Australian men and women who were getting away with heists that made the Great Train Robbery (£2.6 million – about $60 million today) look like peanuts.

'All are accomplished shoplifters who concentrate on departmental stores and jewellers' shops,' the *Gazette* read. 'The method employed by these persons is to visit premises and while the assistants' attention is distracted by some member of the team – making fictitious inquiries – others steal valuable and often bulky items of property.'

Sounds simple and silly enough. You walk into a store, distract the staff and walk out, unnoticed, with jewels worth six figures. Just so.

Melbourne crime reporter Adam Shand, whose book *King of Thieves: The Adventures of Arthur Delaney & the Kangaroo Gang* resurrected the almost-forgotten exploits of the gang, explained in the *Sunday Herald Sun* how it was done; and done over and over again.

> The method relied upon the crooks having a numerical advantage. Three or four 'head pullers' posing as customers would occupy all the staff members. The 'block' would stand in the centre of the shop, hands on his hips so his jacket and

mackintosh fanned out behind him. The block looked like he was a customer waiting to be served but in reality he was Delaney's minder. The 'taker' would slip into the store and move unseen into the blocker's shadow.

Another blocker would keep his body between the first blocker and the taker and be ready to intercept a customer entering the store. With an opened map flapping, the second blocker – often an attractive woman – would ask about how to get to somewhere not too close by. After that it was a matter of taker and first blocker edging their way to a counter, the taker slipping under it to get keys to the showcases and then helping himself. If there was time the taker would rearrange the display so that the missing jewellery was not immediately noticeable. Then the keys were returned and one by one, the gang drifted out of the store. The staff would have no idea they'd been robbed, or – later, when the theft was discovered – who had robbed them.

The key to the gang's success, Adam Shand says, was mobility. 'They had forged passports and international drivers licences. Cheques stolen in London would be cashed in Glasgow within hours. Diamonds stolen in the West End would be sold and re-cut in New York within days.'

By the mid-seventies the Kangaroo Gang was no more. The stores now had closed circuit television that could only be obscured by a blocker three metres tall. Most of the gang had been jailed, been deported or gone back to Australia to continue their careers. 'The Fibber' joined the Grandfather Mob, a team of pension-age criminals who operated during the 1990s robbing courier vans using the distraction method.

The Fibber was 74 when, in 1998, he was found guilty of conspiracy to import drugs – a cannabis haul worth $100 million, seized on a trawler near Hervey Bay. The old boy was sentenced to four years' jail with a minimum of one. Other Kangaroo Gang members, such as Ray Chuck, returned to Melbourne and were linked to the Great Bookie Robbery.

But Arthur Delaney, the Sydney master crook, travelled the world living the high life – he was a devout ladies' man – and carrying on plundering. In June 1990, he robbed Asprey of London, the Queen's jeweller, of almost $10 million in jewels in two daylight robberies. He was never caught and died of a heart attack poolside at a luxury Bangkok hotel three years later.

There is no honour among thieves but the Duke was someone who had won the grudging respect of the Old Bill.

Back in Blighty, Smudger Smith would have dipped his lid to a diamond geezer.

THE GREAT BOOKIE ROBBERY and the Wolf Pack's End

Now this is the Law of the Jungle—as old and as true as the sky;
And the Wolf that shall keep it may prosper, but the Wolf that shall break it must die.
. . .
When ye fight with a Wolf of the Pack, ye must fight him alone and afar,
Lest others take part in the quarrel, and the Pack be diminished by war.

– Rudyard Kipling, 'The Law of the Jungle', from *The Jungle Book* (1894)

Well, Kipling got that right. If only the Kane brothers, Les and Brian, had read his poem and taken it to heart, the wolf pack in the criminal jungle of Melbourne would not have been diminished.

Instead, a brawl in a Melbourne pub, where Brian Kane left most of his left ear in Vinnie Mikkelsen's mouth, ignited an explosion of violence which carried over to the next generation that carried on Melbourne's eternal gang wars.

At the hub of the feud that resulted from both men biting off more than they could chew was the biggest robbery Australia has known: the Great Bookie Robbery.

The Great Bookie Robbery's architect was the charismatic criminal Ray Chuck, later known as Raymond Bennett. The Kane brothers and Bennett were once friends. They grew up street fighting in Melbourne's inner suburbs and graduated to run two gangs. The Kanes, members of the notorious Painters and Dockers Union, lived off rackets on the wharves and standing over other criminals – demanding a share of the loot once the hard work was done. Bennett's gang was best known for armed hold-ups. Both Bennett and the Kanes were thieves and thieves fall out – though seldom as spectacularly as they did in the aftermath of the Great Bookie Robbery.

Bennett went to London in the mid-1970s to join the 'Kangaroo Gang', a loose association of Australian criminals specialising in highly lucrative shoplifting. There he studied and admired the professionalism of the Wembley Mob, an armed hold-up gang who meticulously planned commando-like robberies and whose members could be relied on not to blunder on the job or to break under questioning.

Inspired, Bennett came back to Melbourne and began planning the heist of all heists: an armed robbery at the Victoria Club in Melbourne on a day bookmakers would be settling for not one but three Easter holidays race meetings. He picked his team and gave each man a specific job. One was a time-and-motion expert who believed that the gang could get in and out in not much more than 10 minutes. As well as Bennett, there was Vincent Francis William Mikkelsen, Norman Lee, Ian Revell Carroll, Laurie Prendergast, Anthony Paul McNamara, Dennis William Smith and two armed hold-up specialists. The team went bush on a rigorous 'boot camp' to prepare themselves and in the Easter holidays broke into the empty Victoria Club building for a full dress rehearsal.

On Wednesday, 21 April 1976, dozens of bookies were in the club and cash in 118 calico bags in metal cash boxes had been delivered by a Mayne Nickless armoured truck. Just after midday, a man came to the door saying he was there to fix the refrigerator in the bar. Naturally he was let in immediately. He was followed, however, by six uninvited men wearing balaclavas and carrying submachine guns.

Screaming, 'Everyone on the floor!' they bashed a guard with a gun butt when he reached for his revolver, ripped phones from the wall, cut open cash boxes with bolt cutters and emptied thousands of bank notes into three huge mail sacks.

Eleven minutes later they were out the back door and away. (Police discount the theory that the gang hid the loot upstairs in an office they had rented. That amount of money lying around unattended would be an invitation to a catastrophe. Thieves might get to it. They believe the bags were thrown into a van which was then driven away by Dennis 'Greedy' Smith.)

The heist was colossal; officially, $1.4 million. Unofficially, it may have been worth as much as $15 million at a time when the average annual salary was around $10,000.

The Great Bookie Robbery was hailed in the media as the perfect crime. And it was, but for three little words – 'You too, Ambrose' – when the gang ordered everyone on the floor. These words were rapped out to one of the men at the Victoria Club, Ambrose Palmer, the trainer of the world-champion boxer Johnny Famechon. At once the man behind the balaclava realised he'd made a bad mistake. He'd trained at Palmer's gym and knew Palmer would recognise his voice.

Inevitably the word got out: it was Chuck Bennett's mob. And inevitably the Kanes were anxious to get their unfair share of the haul.

The first salvo in the war was fired at the Richmond pub where Mikkelsen and Brian Kane had a ferocious set to that saw them both end up in hospital. Mikkelsen knew that the Kane brothers would be coming for him and on his behalf Bennett tried to conciliate: he asked the Kanes to forgive Mikkelsen.

> *When Pack meets with Pack in the Jungle, and neither will go from the trail,*
> *Lie down till the leaders have spoken—it may be fair words shall prevail.*
> – Rudyard Kipling, 'The Law of the Jungle', from *The Jungle Book*

Alas, fair words can only take you so far. You can't beat plain speaking and once again the Kane brothers didn't heed Kipling's advice. Their response to Bennett's olive branch was blunt. 'Stick your head in and it will be fucking blown off!'

Bennett's response was even more blunt.

Shortly after, along with Mikkelsen and Laurie Prendergast, Bennett was waiting when Les Kane, his wife Judi and their two young children came home on the night of 19 October 1978. Les put their six-year-old, Martine, to bed as Judi said goodnight to four-year-old Justin. Les went to the bathroom and Judi to their bedroom. She turned on the lights. Three men armed with silenced machine guns were waiting. She screamed: 'Les, look out!' but Kane was busy looking in the mirror, plucking a grey hair from his Zapata moustache.

Kane had time to cry 'Oh, no!' before they shot him, again and again. Judi ran to him while he groaned his last. Then the three men, who had left the house, came back, dragged Kane's torn and bloodied body outside, threw it into the boot of his pink Ford and drove off. Kane's body and the car were never seen again.

Judi Kane identified her husband's killers, breaking the number one unwritten law of the criminal jungle, and the men were sent to trial. But without a body, the case against Bennett, Mikkelsen and Prendergast failed. They were free. For the moment. But now, they knew, it was payback time.

Mikkelsen and Prendergast got out of town at once. Bennett chose to stay in the safety of police custody for the next two months, waiting for his appearance in the Melbourne Magistrates Court for a committal hearing. He was to defend charges over an armed robbery of a $69,000 payroll. Bennett didn't get to give his defence. Instead, with two detectives escorting him, and waiting outside the 19th-century courtroom, he saw a bearded man, with tinted glasses and shoulder-length hair walk up to him and say, 'Cop this, you motherfucker!' as he pulled out a snubnosed revolver and shot him three times.

Bennett staggered as the detectives reeled back. Arms crossed over his chest he gasped, 'I've been shot in the heart!' For crucial moments the police, believing the shooting was faked and that Bennett was about to escape, surrounded him as his legs buckled and he fell. The gunman, meanwhile, rushed out a side door, down back stairs to a gap in a corrugated iron fence that led to a public car park, and vanished. Bennett died within the hour.

His killer was Brian Kane. He lasted almost exactly three years, until November 1982, when he was seated with a woman and a mate at a table at a pub in Lygon Street, and two masked men came in and began firing. Kane sprang to his feet, tipped over the table and made a grab for the woman's handbag. His gun was in it. He didn't get to it.

Kane's death was mourned by many in his community. The Moran clan, three of whom were later shot dead, were at his funeral, as was Alphonse Gangitano, a great admirer of Brian Kane, who followed in his enforcer footsteps and whose 1998 murder by Jason Moran led to more than 30 gangland killings in the following decade.

In time, most of the other members of the Great Bookie Robbery gang followed Bennett and the Kanes, all dying violently.

Mikkelsen escaped retribution, but his innocent brother-in-law was mistakenly shot dead in Mikkelsen's old car. Prendergast was abducted from his car and, like Les Kane, never seen again. Carroll was murdered by a fellow armed bandit. Drug addict McNamara died from an overdose – suspected to be 'hot'. And police shot dead Normie Lee during an attempted armed hold-up at Melbourne Airport in 1992.

On 29 August 2010, the last of the gang went quietly. Broke, a diabetic and an amputee, Dennis 'Greedy' Smith had a heart attack and died in a Melbourne hospital. Also known as 'Fatty', Smith drove the getaway van from the back of the Victoria Club and laundered much of the money overseas. He set up the Aussie Bar in Manila, notorious as a haven for Australian criminals and a meeting point for dealings in drugs and guns.

In his heyday, Smith owned a string of racehorses, gave substantial donations to an Australian Football League club and openly did drug deals from his Rolls-Royce in the streets of Melbourne. Bling flashed from his fat fists; he had gold jewellery worth almost $350,000. He was deported from the Philippines in 1986 and later jailed in Melbourne for 11 years for cocaine trafficking.

Smith was 62 when he died, and with him – probably – the last real link to the Great Bookie Robbery.

THE FRAUDS

Intentional misrepresentation or concealment of information in order to deceive or mislead

FIELD MARSHAL BLAMEY's Inglorious Life

The Field Marshal was dying. Sir Thomas Albert Blamey GBE, KCB, CMG, DSO, ED, had been slowly fading for months and now, in the early hours of 27 May 1951, death claimed him. For some it couldn't have come soon enough.

What were the Field Marshal's last thoughts? Did he wonder had it been worth it – the lies, the bullying, the deceit, the subjugation of rivals, the slur on the courage of the young soldiers on the Kokoda Track, the abandonment of 2400 POWs to a death march from which only five would return? Perhaps he didn't give them any thought. Perhaps, right to the end, as he had done in life, he held to his statement of his early career: 'I do not care much what others think.'

Thomas Blamey was a very vain man but it's true he had little regard for how others saw him. Ambition drove him and he let no man stand in his way if that man could be sidetracked or duped or dumped. Women? They were a different matter. He was all for women standing in his way.

But for the occasional roar of the lions – eerie in the darkness of the city – the Melbourne zoo was quiet that late Friday night in 1936. Outside the zoo, in Lovers Lane, jovial, pot-bellied John Brophy, the Chief of the Criminal Investigation Bureau, sat with a woman friend in the front seat of a parked car. In the back, 'head down' with a naked prostitute, was the Chief Commissioner of the Victoria Police, Brigadier General Sir Thomas Blamey.

Brophy, the man in the front seat, had played a key role in the investigations of the sensational Gun Alley murder in 1921. Seventy-four years on, Kevin Morgan's painstaking research for his book *Gun Alley* revealed that the investigation was crucially flawed and that an innocent man had been hanged. In the course of that research Morgan interviewed 92-year-old Bill Donnelly, who had been at Russell Street Police Headquarters that night in 1936. A former chief of Melbourne's Homicide Squad, Donnelly told Morgan:

> Blamey had compelled Brophy to drive him to the zoo. Blamey and a prostitute were in the back of the Daimler. Brophy and Mrs Orr were in the front. Blamey was drunk and had 'stripped off' the prostitute and had his head 'down' when three men appeared around the car. One man threatened Brophy through an open window on the drivers' side.

According to Donnelly, Brophy pushed him away and the man fell to the ground. Brophy wound up the window. The man on the ground 'growled like a dog' and pulled out a gun, wounding Brophy with three shots.

This 2005 disclosure contradicts the official line that persisted for seven decades. Blamey's most recent biographer, David Horner, in *Blamey the Commander-in-Chief*, for instance, wrote that Brophy was waiting to meet an informer.

Also in the car were two women and a driver. Suddenly two masked and armed men attempted to hold up the occupants of the car. Brophy drew his pistol and fired two shots but was himself shot three times. The other occupants of the car were unharmed, the bandits escaped and Brophy was taken to St Vincent's Hospital.

Although there was no suggestion of any immoral behaviour concerning the women who were respectable members of the Melbourne community, Brophy was anxious for their involvement not to become known to the press. In the morning Blamey visited the hospital, and information was later released to the press that Brophy had accidentally shot himself [three times!] while handling his pistol.

This version has more holes in it than the much-ventilated John Brophy. What was the head of the CIB doing meeting an informer late at night with two women – 'respectable members of the Melbourne community' – and a driver in a car parked in Lovers Lane? And how could a senior policeman shoot himself three times?

That evening's *Herald* broke the news that Brophy had been shot by thugs, but didn't mention the respectable women. By Monday, Blamey, who announced that Brophy had shot himself, now claimed that it was Brophy who had told him it was an accident – or three. And once again the respectable women were left out of the story. A Royal Commission called into the matter found that Brophy had told Blamey the true story of the shooting but that Blamey, to hide the fact that two women were in the car and 'being jealous of the reputation of the force he [Blamey] commands', had given 'replies which were not in accordance with the truth'.

Blamey was forced to resign. He might have survived (the real facts of his role in the shooting still unknown) if it had not been for the scandalous affair of Badge 80 seven years earlier. Together, the two dark doings did for him.

The Badge 80 affair began around midnight on 21 October 1925, when three plain-clothes Licensing Squad policemen knocked on the terrace house door of a brothel in Fitzroy, Melbourne. Inside, they had reason to believe, sly grog was being sold on the premises. Women sold their bodies on the premises, too, but that was nothing to do with the Licensing Squad. Nonetheless, it was a chance to have a squiz.

Upstairs they opened a bedroom door and saw a couple 'in a state of undress'. The man, short and stocky and with a moustache, allegedly said, in the robotic language that only policemen employ: 'That is alright, boys. I am a plain-clothes constable. Here is my badge.' And he showed them a medal with the number 80. He did not identify himself.

So that was alright then.

Back at headquarters, the police found that police badge number 80 belonged to General Thomas Blamey, the Chief Commissioner of Police in Victoria. So that wasn't alright. Questions were asked in Parliament and the Government quickly cleared up the matter:

> Inspecting Superintendent Warren investigated the matter and found that the medal was, prior to the date of the raid, in some way removed from the possession of the Chief Commissioner of Police ... The medal was surreptitiously returned to General Blamey. [It had been left, thoughtfully, in General Blamey's letterbox at the Naval and Military Club in Little Collins Street.] Every effort has been made to establish the identity of the person who used the medal on this occasion and to trace the person responsible for the theft, but without success. It has, however, been conclusively proved that it was not used by General Blamey.

So that was alright then.

Well, no. 'Even an infant-in-arms can plainly see that [Blamey] himself was there in person, but naturally his subordinates dare not say so openly,' an anonymous correspondent wrote to the Premier. 'The defence of the stolen badge is so thin that not even an imbecile would be deceived, and in the interests of common decency it was your simple duty to order an enquiry, for what efficiency can one expect from a police force with such a man at its head?'

The Chief Secretary considered whether an enquiry was needed and asked Blamey what he thought. Blamey thought it was better for two detectives to look into the matter. They found that Blamey was not the man with the number 80 badge on the night of the raid. Furthermore, an old army friend of the General was able to confirm that on the night of the raid Blamey was at home. Blamey told the Chief Secretary, in strictest confidence, that he had given his keyring, with its badge, to another old army chum from Sydney so that he could get some alcohol in Blamey's locker at the Naval and Military Club. The chum apparently had no compunctions about waving the number 80 badge at the licensing police, but Blamey, always compassionate, refused to name him because he was a married man, the father of three little kiddies.

There was some small glitch with Blamey's story. Superintendent David Linehan told the investigators that he had seen the badge on Blamey's desk late on the afternoon of the raid on the brothel. Blamey had said the medal had gone missing two days before. The Chief Secretary weighed up Linehan's claim and concluded it was 'disloyal'. The detectives investigating the mystery said it would have been easy to take the medal from Blamey's office and even easier to return it to pigeonholes or boxes at the Naval and Military Club, where it turned up soon after the raid. And Mabel Tracey, the brothel Madam, had no idea who the man with the medal had been – except that it was not the Chief Commissioner.

So that was alright then, though the odium never left the General.

Blamey's 11 years as Chief Commissioner of the Victoria Police were often controversial.

In 1928, waterside workers in Melbourne went on strike. Volunteer strikebreakers brought in were threatened with murder, homes were bombed and on 2 November the escalating violence peaked when police opened fire on the strikers, injuring several and killing one, a Gallipoli veteran. Blamey defended the police and took no action against his men: 'Had the police failed to fire on the mob, which was already attacking them with missiles, and thus failed to protect the bureau labourers, they would have failed in their duty.'

Three years later, at the height of the Great Depression, Blamey ordered that police use batons on the heads of unemployed marchers causing a breach of the peace. At the same time he may have been the head of a secret army, the far right patriotic League of National Security, formed in Victoria. Said to be led by 'a high military officer' the LNS had thousands of members – one estimate reckoned 30,000 – and like the New Guard in Sydney, it was ready to take arms in times of a left-wing or communist uprising. Blamey, fiercely anti-communist, is believed by many to have been the 'high military officer' who, at the same time as he headed the Victoria Police Force, led the secret army.

Opinions differ about Blamey's abilities as a general. That is to be expected of any military leader. But Blamey was a bully and a liar, a man who had no difficulty reconciling his taste for prostitutes with the standards expected of a police commissioner or an Australia's supreme commander during World War II. He saw no incompatibility with his private behaviour and his high position. Putting it politely, he was a bounder. Those who fought on the Kokoda Track and those 2400 who died on the Sandakan death marches would have put it more bluntly. For all the letters after his name those men would have awarded him only one honorific: Bastard of the First Order.

Blamey's scandalous past as Police Commissioner is already almost forgotten. But in 1942, his insulting condemnation of the men who some say had saved Australia – implying they were cowards – will always be remembered. Blamey's aide-de-camp, Norman Carlyon, in his biography *I Remember Blamey*, gives this sanitised account of a despicable attack.

> I well remember one example of Blamey's close attention to the performance of his fighting men. It concerned the 21st Brigade after a setback in their thrust forward from Ioribai Ridge [Papua New Guinea].
>
> This brigade, which had a fine record in the Middle East, was fighting its first jungle action. When the flanks were infiltrated by the enemy, the brigade made a limited retirement. This was a successful operation in which very few casualties were suffered. However this check displeased Blamey. He ordered the entire brigade be paraded at Koitaki so that he could address them.

Five weeks before Blamey's arrival at Koitaki, Major General 'Tubby' Allen, who, grossly unfairly, Blamey was soon to sack, had reviewed the brigade and congratulated them on their achievements on the Kokoda Track. The men now on parade presumed Blamey was about to do the same.

Norman Carlyon wrote:

> Standing beside the small platform from which Blamey was to address the troops, I realised that he was in a most aggressive mood. He was soon expressing this in harsh words.
>
> He told the men that they had been defeated and Australia had been defeated. He said this was not good enough. Every

soldier there had to remember he was worth three Japanese. [Blamey held the view that the Japanese were half human, half ape.] In future he expected no further retirements but advance at all costs. He concluded with a remark which I think was particularly ill chosen and unfair . . . 'Remember,' he said, 'it is not the man with the gun that gets shot, it's the rabbit that is running away.'

The men were outraged. Some later said Blamey was lucky to escape with his life. Padre Fred Burt and other officers refused to go to a meeting with Blamey and one swung a punch at Carlyon. Later that year, in Perth, Padre Burt met the adjutant general, Major General Lloyd. When Lloyd put it to Burt that Blamey's remarks were a mistake and mistakes were made in any campaign Burt replied: 'On this occasion the men who saved Australia in spite of your mistakes are the men who are blamed.' Burt turned his back on Lloyd and walked away.

In April 1945, in a nationwide broadcast, Blamey said, 'In no other country have the achievements of a very successful army been so belittled as in Australia.' A curious statement coming from the man who had so despicably belittled his own troops. Of course, being Blamey, he may have meant that his own reputation as the supreme commander of the very successful army had been belittled. But if he meant it as a sop, a half-apology to the troops in Papua New Guinea, it was far too little a sop and far too late.

At Sandakan he wasn't late. He just wasn't there when his men desperately needed him. One of them, Private Nelson Short, 2/18th Battalion, remembered listening to the Japanese interpreter telling the skeletal prisoners: 'All men who can stand on their feet be prepared to march.' At the same time an Allied aircraft, 'a monstrous Catalina flying boat' flew overhead, 'You could see the airmen looking down at us. No shot was fired. I often wondered about that.'

Private Short was one of 2400 men, Australian and British, in the camp at Sandakan, a town on the north-east coast of Borneo. He and five others came out alive. The rest died; around half of starvation, dysentery, beriberi or malaria. The rest were murdered – tortured beyond endurance, bayoneted, bashed with rifle butts or shot.

When Private Short saw the Catalina flying over the Sandakan camp he and the Japanese knew that the Allies were likely to land at any moment. It was late January 1945 and the Japanese, knowing that they were losing the war, were determined that their prisoners would not be liberated. And, but for six men of the 2400 they weren't.

Could they have been rescued?

Blamey claimed, when questions were raised after the war, that plans were made to parachute troops into Sandakan, free the POWs and overrun the area but, 'at the moment we wanted to act we couldn't get the necessary aircraft to take them in'.

Lynette Silver, an Australian historian and the foremost expert on the Sandakan death marches, dismisses this. The failure, she says, was due to poor decision making and a series of bungles. 'Blamey lied and blamed others,' she says.

As he had done throughout his life. His public lies had begun in 1900 when, as a 16-year-old pupil-teacher at a school near Wagga Wagga he hit a boy across the face with a ruler. When the boy's father and the head teacher confronted him, Blamey denied it. Years later he agreed he hit the boy but said, 'I couldn't admit it.' As Police Commissioner, as supreme commander, his career and his ego always came first when it came to the truth.

So, were Thomas Blamey's last thoughts of Sandakan and of Koitaki, of the women and the grog? Unlikely. Perhaps, in his last moments, he thought of the poem he wrote as a deeply religious 19-year-old, struggling with the darker side of his nature that would, as he suspected, overwhelm him:

O Lord lead thou me on
I grope and struggle in my darkness Lord,
And seek for that my soul has long adored,
Lead thou me on,
Through earthmists dark and void,
Lead thou me on.

Perhaps these were his last thoughts.
   Perhaps.

ALAN BOND and the Lost Billions

He was our national hero, an entrepreneur who strutted the world stage, who mesmerised all with that Grand Canyon smile ... medical experts were called to testify that Bond was a brain-dead ignoramus who could not take the stand ... A couple of days before he was released after less than four years in jail for fraud involving $1.2 billion, a Northern Territory man was sentenced to one year's jail for stealing $23 worth of cordial and biscuits. Had the same formula been applied to Bond, he would have been in jail for 50 million years.

— Sydney Morning Herald, 7 October 2000

You'd have to have a heart of stone not to laugh. There on the front pages and leading the nightly television news was Alan Bond, leaving after another tough day in court. Bewildered, eyes fighting back the anguish, he was pitiful. And limping. Limping like a weather-beaten old pirate making his way uphill to the George and Dragon after too many years of yo-ho-ho-ing and too much plunder.

Alan Bond's legal team, surrounding him with matching worried mien, insisted that his limp was the result of severe depression. But other, unkind souls, said Bondy's gait would have improved markedly if he'd taken the trouble to empty his shoe of the large pebble it surely held.

Cynics have always been cruel to Alan Bond. 'Some people think they can say what they like about me . . .Well, it hurts, I can tell you. It hurts,' he complained. 'I'd just ask people: "Isn't it about time they gave Alan Bond a fair go?"'

Bond, who has fathomless chutzpah, went on Andrew Denton's *Enough Rope* to talk about the cynics and his colourful career. Denton, the finest and funniest interviewer Australian television has known, began: 'Whenever I mention to people, "I'm interviewing Alan Bond," they say, "Oh, has he got his memory back?" Because they remember you from those court cases in 1994 where you were apparently very, very sick. How sick were you?'

These days Alan Bond seems to have regained his memory, is reputed to be worth $60 million despite the hundreds of millions he owes, and lives in a penthouse in London with his second wife, Diana Bliss.

Alan Bond was the most egregious of the corporate cowboys – 'Last Resort' Laurie Connell, Robert Holmes à Court, Christopher Skase, George Herscu, Abe Goldberg, Larry Adler and the like – dodgy high-flyers on the Australian financial landscape over the last quarter of a century. Most of them were patently unpalatable. But for a time, Alan Bond was the Australian Idol.

The man who financed our successful America's Cup Challenge, Bondy seemed to have no limit to his imagination or his purse. (The reality was, of course, that winning the unwinnable America's Cup gave Bond the credentials he needed to borrow huge amounts from the Western Australian state government and the banks, whose generosity to men like Bond – $28 billion, all of it lost – was boundless.)

At the height of his entrepreneurial career his public company Bond Group and his private company Dallhold owned major breweries in Australia and North America, the Nine television network,

West Australian newspapers, property developments, mining operations, the discount chain Norman Ross and the department store chain Waltons, Thorn EMI film studios, New York's swish St Moritz hotel, and most of an English village.

The newspaper image sums it up: Bond, photographed from outside his Swan Airship is seen in the capacious cabin, grinning through the window, sumptuous meals on the table before him, while behind him brewery execs, beer cans in hand like Bond, beam with the wonder of it all.

Bondy was garrulous and gregarious, unlike his fellow Western Australian entrepreneur Robert Holmes à Court, a man who, Les Carlyon wrote, 'spoke the way pharmacists used to dispense arsenic: carefully, slowly, every syllable weighed. He seldom said what he meant or finished a sentence.'

Bondy, for his part, loved the limelight. He was photographed with prime ministers and the Pope, and he was president of the Richmond Football Club: proof positive that Bondy was a dinki-di Aussie who just happened to be a billionaire.

But that was before the Bond Corporation's $8.23 billion crash. 'Tiny' Rowland, a tough and shrewd English businessman – whose conglomerate, Lonrho, faced a takeover by Bond – precipitated the fall. The Bond Corporation and Bond himself were then at the height of their fame. Bond had just – supposedly – paid $53 million for a not particularly good Van Gogh, and he seemed set to assume the throne of the emperor of international commerce.

Tiny Rowland said the emperor had no clothes. Or if he had, they were threadbare.

People began looking closely at the emperor, and shortly after Tiny Rowland's view was confirmed. Bond Corporation went into receivership. Alan Bond was declared bankrupt, paying his personal creditors $3.25 million to settle debts of more than half a billion.

In 1992 he was jailed for 30 months for dishonesty, released after a retrial but then jailed for three years over some creative accounting involving another very costly work of art. He was jailed for a further four years in 1997 for deception to the tune of $1.2 billion. It was at this trial that he claimed to be suffering from amnesia caused by depression and brain damage. On appeal by the Crown the sentence was increased to seven years, but the High Court overturned that sentence on a technicality and Bond was released on parole.

In 2003 in Perth Bondy was back in the spotlight, part of the 20th anniversary celebrations of the America's Cup win.

Paul Barry, who so incensed Bond that, on camera, he tore up Barry's media pass, wrote that, 'For 20 years Alan Bond plundered his public companies . . . at the end of it he left a black hole of around five billion Australian dollars which was losses borne by shareholders, creditors, bankers and the rest . . . He then managed to hang on to a private fortune of something like $100 million . . . what he did in the 1980s and the 1990s was a disgrace to this country and he brought us into disrepute around the world . . . he made a fool of the legal system and he made a fool of all of us too.'

That's why most people don't think it's about time to give Alan Bond a fair go.

THE *TRIAL* and the Treachery

'It is a truth universally acknowledged,' as Jane Austen's father might have told her, 'that a ship in possession of a good fortune must be in want of plundering.'

The *Trial* was such a ship. It carried a treasure in gold spangles and doubloons destined for the King of Siam when it struck a rock off the west coast of Australia on the night of 25 May 1622 and went down with the loss of 93 men.

The *Trial* was the first English ship to sight Australia, and the first ship known to be wrecked off the Australian coast. But what followed was an old story: a dark and despicable story of greed and treachery that was echoed 350 years later, deep in the *Trial*'s Indian Ocean tomb.

The *Trial*'s captain, John Brookes, was acknowledged to have behaved in a cowardly way when his ship struck: he left most of his crew to die and sailed to safety in Java. But in 1934 a woman researching the wreck turned the shipwreck tragedy into a detective story that revealed Brookes was much more than a coward: he was one of the great villains of maritime history.

The *Trial*, owned by the British East India Company and captained by Brookes, sailed from Plymouth on 4 September 1621 with a crew of 143 'good men' and a chart based on the 'Brouwer Route' to the East Indies.

Ten years before, Brouwer, a Dutch seaman, had shown that the best way to the Indies and the Javanese capital of Batavia (Jakarta) was to sail due east in the lower latitudes from the Cape of Good Hope, before turning north some several hundred nautical miles before the Great South Land was reached. This route gave his ship favourable and reliable winds – the Roaring Forties – and was considerably faster and healthier than following Vasco da Gama's diagonal route up the east coast of Africa and across the Indian Ocean, which often left ships becalmed under the searing tropical heat, their crews rotting from disease. Following the new route too far east, however, meant encountering what Dirk Hartog called 'a large land mass' – the west coast of Australia. He became the first man to do so, at Cape Inscription on 25 October 1616.

In 1620 an English ship captained by Humphrey Fitzherbert had followed the Brouwer route and when, the following year, the merchant ship the *Trial* set out for the Indies the Company instructed Brookes to set its course from Fitzherbert's log. The British East India Company was bent on wresting the lucrative spice trade from the Dutch United East India Company, and the *Trial* was well named.

Brookes was a poor navigator. He sailed too far east and on 1 May sighted the Australian mainland in the vicinity of North West Cape. For weeks strong winds prevented the *Trial* from heading north for Java, but on 24 May the winds changed, allowing for progress north past Barrow Island and the Monte Bello Islands. On 25 May 1622, eight weeks after the *Trial* left the Cape, Captain Brookes had his ship, as he later reported to the British East India Company, steering 'north east thinking to fall in with the western part of Java'.

Instead the *Trial* fell in on a pinnacle of rock, an uncharted reef. Brookes wrote:

> At 11 o'clock at night, fair weather and smooth the ship struck. I cried to them to bear up and tack to the westwards. They did their best, but the rock being sharp the ship was presently full of water . . . The wind began suddenly to freshen and to blow. I struck round my sails and got out my skiff and . . . made all the way I could to get out my long boat and by two o'clock I had gotten her out and hanged her in the tackles on the side.
>
> Seeing the ship full of water and the wind to increase [I] made all the means I could to save my life and as many of my company as I could. The boat put off at four in the morning and half an hour after the fore part of the ship fell in pieces! Ten men were saved in the skiff and 36 in the longboat.

That left 93 men on board the disintegrating *Trial*. (Four men had died on the voyage.) And Captain Brookes' account also left out most of the truth of what happened when the *Trial* struck – and where and why.

The truth about Captain Brookes was disclosed by a man named Thomas Bright who sailed on the ship and whose letter detailing the events that followed the shipwreck was filed and forgotten for three centuries. Bright was the British East India Company's agent on board the *Trial*. His unsigned letter to a senior officer of the company tells how the captain wrecked his ship, abandoned most of his crew to certain death and, with the treasure, escaped on a skiff with his cabin boy and a chosen few.

> May the 25th, about ten o'clock at night, fair weather and little wind, the ship Tryall, by carelessness for want of looking out, struck upon the rocks . . . her hold full of water in an instant . . . [Brookes'] crew and fellow and consorts providing provisions and saving his things, bearing Mr Jackson and myself with fair words, promising us faithfully to take us along.

Then, 'like a Judas' while Bright had his back to him in the captain's cabin, Brookes slipped way and lowered himself into the skiff 'only with nine men and his boy. [He] stood for the Straits of Sunda that instant, without care and without seeing the lamentable end of the ship, the time she split, or respect of any man's life.'

Bright and 35 others got the longboat out with difficulty and stood off until dawn when the men remaining alive on the ship were left to their doom, the waters now crashing over the remains of the *Trial* and the sharks busy.

Brookes' skiff had a keg of water, two cases of bottles of wine and a little bread and 1500 kilometres of water between it and Java, but they made it to Batavia. So too did the 36 men on Bright's longboat, surviving on six kegs of water, a little wine and some bread.

In Batavia, Brookes wrote his official report on the disaster. To escape all blame he falsified the ship's position and said that the Trial Rocks, as they were soon known, were many kilometres west – a lie that led seamen from Dampier to Flinders to search fruitlessly for the reef for the next 200 years.

Brookes also told the company that he had transferred the ship's treasure to Bright in the longboat. Bright's report disagreed: '... for two hours [he did] nothing but convey from his cabin to his skiff to my knowledge both letters, money and spangles in his trunk ...'

Despite this damning letter, Brookes' story was believed. The following year he was given command of the *Moone* and wrecked it off the coast of England. He and the master were imprisoned, charged with deliberately wrecking the ship and stealing the jewels and diamonds in the chest of a company official who had died during the voyage. Once again, Brookes' story was believed: he was given a reward of £10 plus wages for his cabin boy, who had stolen the jewels but then returned them to the company.

But he never returned the treasure of the King of Siam.

It took almost 350 years to discover the true site of the wreck of the *Trial*. In 1969 a group of Perth divers travelled 1500 kilometres north to attempt to find it. The wreck, they believed, had been pinpointed by brilliant research done in 1934 that uncovered Bright's damning private letter.

'Ida Leigh Marriott did the original research,' Jeremy Green, head of the Western Australian Museum's Department of Maritime Archaeology told the ABC in 2003.

'She looked at Brookes' journal and Bright's journal and put the story together and said this is clearly the Monte Bellos and this is clearly Barrow Island, and the Trial Rocks by that point had been charted halfway between the Monte Bellos and Barrow Island and she spotted it as being these rocks up in the north which we actually called Ritchie's Reef, so these guys went up there – a very difficult place to dive – and were lucky enough to get on the site and found the cannon and anchors.'

Green himself did the dive two years later. He found there had been an attempt to plunder the *Trial*, just as there had been three centuries before.

'The first museum dive on the site – when we got there – we found it had been blown up. There were explosives all over the place, and there were detonator cords and pieces of gelignite. Somebody had got in there, and it was in fact Alan Robinson.'

Ellis Alfred 'Alan' Robinson was one of the team that found the *Trial*. A violent man, he is believed to have carried out the blasting some time shortly before Green's dive, working from a trawler. He was charged but, like Brookes, acquitted. Robinson is thought to have plundered other famous wrecks along the coast, among them the notorious *Batavia*, the 700 ton *Zuytdorp*, and the flagship of the Dutch fleet, the *Vergulde Draek* (Gilt Dragon), sunk with 78,000 gold guilders.

In 1983, on trial for conspiring to murder his de facto partner, using explosives and acid, he died, probably by his own hand.

The Dirty Double Dealings of
AL GRASSBY

If, one sunny Saturday morning in Flash Al's Car Mart you saw, weaving his way towards you, a short man clad in a lilac suit teamed with a sunset kipper tie, his hair dyed jet black, sporting the moustache of a cartoon spiv, and giggling through a smile that a crocodile would kill for, you'd back off as quickly and as decently as you could, all the while keeping a firm grip on your wallet.

To be fair to Al Grassby, we can all agree on that.

But there are areas of disagreement. Al Grassby's name is invariably linked with the adjectives 'colourful' and 'controversial', and almost always the phrase 'father of multiculturalism'. He was colourful, no question. And he was controversial, at times, though he enjoyed a free ride from most of the media for the majority of his career. He was not, however, although he liked the title, the father of multiculturalism. Al Grassby was a criminal. He was crooked. Deeply and wickedly corrupt.

Was Grassby the father of multiculturalism? That title belongs to an advisor to the Whitlam, Fraser and then Howard governments who helped develop Australia's multicultural policies. In May 2009, the ABC's Peter Cave announced, 'The father of multiculturalism in Australia, Jerzy Zubrzycki has died . . . Rather than a melting pot, he believed that immigration policies should reflect people from different cultures, sharing one political structure.' Zubrzycki didn't even like the word multiculturalism. James Jupp, a fellow academic at Australian National University said, 'His particular concern was what he called cultural pluralism, that is the retaining the languages particularly of Europeans. So he didn't actually like the word multiculturalism himself. He blamed that on Al Grassby.' Grassby himself preferred the term polyethnicity, which was never going to take off.

Everything about Flash Al was false, from the tip of his dyed hair to the name he went by. He falsely presented himself as a happily married man, an Italian or at least a Mediterranean. In Parliament he represented Riverina farmers, but in reality he represented Griffith marijuana growers. And yet the media, who knew or suspected this, found him amusing – good copy. And Grassby, until he went to trial, charged with criminal defamation, played them for the suckers they were.

At his trial, however, the media heard how he had tried – again and again – to implicate an innocent woman, Barbara Mackay, her son and her solicitor in the murder of her husband, Donald Mackay. On Grassby's death in 2005, we learned what the trial and libel laws had kept from us: that he had allegedly been paid $40,000 to do this by the men who ordered Donald Mackay's murder – the Griffith Calabrian criminal network. It was said that he had been on their payroll for 40 years.

By and large the obituaries for Grassby were kind. Paul Heinrichs in the *Age* asked whether he was 'father of multiculturalism, or just a colourful lair from Griffith?' and concluded 'he was a bit of both and then some'. Heinrichs allowed that there had been some bumps along the journey: 'But times became tougher for Grassby, who had grown close to many of the Italian families of Griffith, not all of whom were law-abiding Calabrians.'

Mungo MacCallum in the *Sydney Morning Herald* was a

little more forthright: Grassby, he said, passionately defended 'the extended "family" of Robert Trimbole, who had ordered Mackay's murder, but when Grassby maintained that it was somehow Mackay's fault, or at least that of his family . . . This did not go down well.' That was one way of putting it.

'He is survived by Ellnor, their daughter Gabriella, a grandson, and his partner, Angela Chan,' MacCallum concluded. Discerning obituary readers would have noticed the sting in the tail here. So if Angela was Grassby's partner, who was Ellnor?

Keith Moor, the respected Melbourne *Herald Sun* investigator, told the story of the two women in Grassby's life. He had spent the last 25 years of his life sharing himself between them, Moor reported, Angela in Sydney and Ellnor in Canberra: 'To the haunting lament of an Irish piper, flamboyant "father of multiculturalism" Al Grassby was farewelled from this world two Fridays ago by his devoted wife of 43 years, Ellnor, at St Christopher's Cathedral in Canberra. Six days later, to the romantic strumming of a flamenco guitar at St Patrick's Church in Sydney, Angela Chan, Grassby's self-described partner of 25 years, tearfully farewelled her "inspiration and champion".'

The two women and their diverse musical tastes were all part of the double stitching in the tapestry of Al Grassby's life.

Albert Jaime Grass was born in Brisbane in 1926 to an Irish mother and a Spanish father. He changed his surname to Grassby, it's said, to emphasise his Irish roots. To be sure, to be sure. More likely he wanted it to have an Italian flavour, since he looked like a Neapolitan gelati vendor, something that stood him in good stead when he set his sights on a career in politics. In 1965, standing for Labor he won Murrumbidgee and entered the New South Wales Parliament. In the landmark federal election four years later he won the Riverina electorate, with its strong Italian constituency.

In 1972, Gough Whitlam appointed him the Minister for

Immigration. However, while he revelled in the limelight and the laughter as the colourful character Flash Al, he raised eyebrows with a trip to Plati, an Italian town with a population of around 3000. Plati was the stronghold of the Calabrian version of the Mafia – the Honoured Society. Many of the Italians in Griffith had come from Plati, and Grassby used his ministerial discretion to grant Australian entry visas to three Plati men who had been deported from Australia or refused entry because of their criminal records.

In May 1974, Grassby lost his seat, partly as a result of the preference votes directed by the Liberal Party candidate, Donald Mackay, to the successful National Party candidate, John Sullivan.

Whitlam then made Grassby the first federal Commissioner for Community Relations. Here he worked tirelessly for such people as Juni Morosi, a stunning beauty from the Philippines. Grassby appointed Morosi as his assistant and introduced her to a number of Labor politicians, including Deputy Prime Minister Jim Cairns, and the Attorney-General Lionel Murphy. Murphy wrote a letter, later leaked, to ACT Minister Gordon Bryant seeking preferential housing treatment for Morosi. The media uproar put Morosi in a spotlight from which she backed out only after the end of her affair with the Deputy Prime Minister and the fall of the Labor Government.

Keith Moor's revelations focused on Grassby's criminal life and quoted Bruce Provost, a retired senior investigator with the National Crime Authority. Provost told Moor he had no doubt that Grassby was paid to commit crimes and do favours for the Calabrian Honoured Society and that Grassby had used political pressure to block an investigation into his links with it.

The stench about the disappearance of Donald Mackay and the failure of the police to find his killers finally led to an investigation, 10 years after the murder. Justice Nagle's Special Inquiry into the Police Investigation into the Death of Donald Bruce Mackay reported:

On 1 June 1983, [Frank] Tizzone [a Mafia 'supergrass'] made a 17-page statement to Victoria Police. In it, he said that he had been present at a meeting in 1977 at Griffith with Tony Sergi [a close friend of Grassby's], Tony Barbaro and Robert Trimbole, at which Mackay and the difficulties created by his anti-drug crusade were discussed.

At this meeting, three possible alternatives were mentioned as a means of ending Mackay's harassment of their business: the first was to buy his silence, the second to compromise him with a woman, and the third, to murder him. Two days later, on 3 June 1983, Tizzone retracted this part of his statement and confined his remarks to an agreement reached in Melbourne between himself and George Joseph, a Melbourne gun dealer and the 'hit man', Bazley, to kill Mackay. The agreement to kill Mackay originated from an earlier request by Robert Trimbole to Tizzone to procure a hired assassin. Tizzone claimed that at a much later date arrangements were made for the same man, Bazley, to murder Mr Asia heroin couriers Douglas and Isabel Wilson.

On Friday 15 July, Nagle reported:

Mackay left his furniture store at approximately 5.30 to 5.40 pm and drove a minivan belonging to the store into the parking area of the Griffith Hotel. He parked this vehicle with its nose towards the fence furthest from the hotel buildings, and about two-thirds of the way along the parking area from the Yambil Street entrance . . . Mackay left the Griffith Hotel at about 6.30 pm, and was not seen again. About the same time, Roy Laurence Binks, an accountant in his premises which had a common wall with the Griffith Hotel car park, heard three noises similar to the cracking of a whip and, twice, two or three seconds apart, a noise like someone being 'sick or vomiting and similar to a groan'.

Donald Mackay's body was never recovered.

About Grassby's reported attempts to publicise a four-page document suggesting that those responsible for Mackay's murder were his wife, his son and his solicitor Ian Salmon, Nagle had this to say: 'The Commission makes only one comment – that no decent man could have regarded the general attacks on the Calabrians as justifying him in propagating the scurrilous lies contained in the anonymous document.'

Grassby resigned from the $48,000-a-year community post Neville Wran had given him in 1986. In 1987, the National Crimes Authority charged him with conspiring with Robert Trimbole and others to pervert the course of justice. He was also charged with criminal defamation of Barbara Mackay, Paul Donald Mackay and Ian Salmon. The cases dragged on for 12 years until in 1992 Grassby was acquitted, the NSW Court of Criminal Appeal saying that guilty verdicts against Grassby looked like compromises rather than verdicts and did not make legal or logical sense. Grassby was awarded costs of $180,000. Barbara Mackay had earlier sued Grassby for defamation and won.

Years later, Donald Mackay's son Paul, on behalf of his family, wrote a letter to the *Canberra Times*, protesting, in vain, against the bizarre decision by Jon Stanhope, Labor's Chief Minister for the Australian Capital Territory, to honour Grassby with a life-size statue:

> Commissioner Nagle noted that he found Grassby's evidence to be unconvincing and constantly driven to uneasy claims of defective memory.
>
> While immigration minister, Grassby abused his power by issuing visas to mafia figures who had previously been deported from Australia because of their criminal records.
>
> We feel that Grassby is an inappropriate choice to represent the hard work and integrity of the people who came to make

a new life in Australia. There are many immigrants from the Canberra community far more deserving of such an accolade.

Today, in Canberra, the man is commemorated, advancing on you, arms outstretched and smiling egregiously, as though welcoming you to Multicultural Land. And though Flash Al Grassby is dead, your first impulse, still, is to back away clutching your wallet.

MARCUS EINFELD: The Hubris of a Living Legend

Open on title: Jerry Seinfeld, superimposed on exterior of downtown Manhattan apartment block.
SOUND EFFECTS: *Theme music, bass twang.*
Cut to interior, Seinfeld's apartment. George is explaining to Jerry and Elaine that he's found a foolproof way to avoid his latest traffic fine.
ELAINE: *You mean I've got to go to Australia so you don't have to pay a lousy $77 fine?*
GEORGE: *No! That's the beauty of it. All I do is tell 'em you had my car that day and then you went to Australia and that they can't contact you because you're dead. You were killed in a car accident.*
ELAINE: *I'm dead in Australia?!*
Cut to the door. Kramer bursts in and overhears this.
KRAMER *(pointing triumphantly at George): The Costanza Defence!*
Cut to George smirking.
ELAINE: *The Costanza Defence. You guys have done this before?*
GEORGE *(smugly): Works every time.*

Cut to Jerry shaking his head in wonderment. His small smile tells us that any minute this is going to get out of control. Big time.
SOUND EFFECTS: The intercom buzzes.
Jerry picks up the intercom phone.
VOICE-OVER: Police. Do you have a George Costanza up there?

Marcus Einfeld AO, was seated in Court 13A of the New South Wales Supreme Court on 19 March 2009. Proclaimed a Living National Treasure in 1997, Marcus Einfeld had been a justice of the Federal Court of Australia and the Supreme Courts of NSW, Western Australia and the Australian Capital Territory; a Unicef Ambassador for Children; Austcare's Ambassador for Refugees; National Vice President of the International Commission of Jurists; Foundation President of the Australian Human Rights and Equal Opportunity Commission . . . well the list of achievements and titles and awards just goes on and on.

His entry in *Who's Who* that year ran to 54 lines, around 450 words. The then Prime Minister, John Howard had an entry just over half that length. Entries in *Who's Who* are written by the subject. *Who's Who* trusts the author's honesty. And there is the key to Marcus Richard Einfeld's presence in Court 13A on 19 March 2009.

Marcus Einfeld had often been in the NSW Supreme Court. But never before had he been in the dock. Seated, his head down, his face in his hands, his eyes closed, he looked up only when he heard Justice Bruce James sentence him to three years in prison for perjury and for attempting to pervert the course of justice, charges he pleaded guilty to.

And all because he lied – foolish lies, over and over – to avoid a $77 speeding fine.

Einfeld had a history of beating speeding and traffic signal violations. Three times before 8 January 2006, when a speed camera in Mosman registered his car doing 60 kilometres an hour in a 50 kilometres an hour zone, he had been caught speeding or running red lights. Each time he came up with what legal and media circles came to refer to as the Einfeld Defence: he hadn't been the driver of his car; instead it had been driven by friends who were not in the country.

And it worked. The Einfeld Defence, of course, rested on his reputation. It was unthinkable that a man who had been a Federal Court judge, a justice of the NSW Supreme Court, as he had been, would lie over such a paltry matter. But then he tried it a fourth time.

After getting the Mosman speeding notice Einfeld made a statutory declaration. He nominated a Professor Teresa Brennan as the person 'in control' of the car and elected to have the matter heard by a magistrate. On 7 August 2006, he gave sworn evidence in court that he had left Sydney to go to Forster on 6 January 2006, two days before the offence. He had lent his car to an old friend, Professor Brennan.

Case dismissed. But inevitably the snickers that the case caused among those in the know reached the media. A *Daily Telegraph* journalist began digging. Professor Teresa Brennan, the journalist found, had been killed in a car accident in Florida three years before.

Questioned by the *Telegraph*, Einfeld came up with a bizarre explanation. He knew two Professor Teresa Brennans, he said. Both were Australians and both had died in motor accidents in the United States. The Teresa Brennan who had been driving his car early in the year was not the Teresa Brennan killed three years before.

The Living National Treasure, a man frequently quoted on the moral issues of illegal immigration, was also known as Marcus

Minefield and Marcus Seinfeld. And now he was living up to those names. Police began investigating whether Einfeld had committed perjury.

Now his story changed. He left his trip to Forster out of the scenario. Instead, he said that he had lent his car to Brennan, and that he had suddenly remembered he was to meet a friend at a Pittwater restaurant and had borrowed his mother's car.

Einfeld was angered when asked on the ABC's *Four Corners* if he was dishonest. 'That's a bit offensive and I don't think I'm in the slightest bit dishonest,' he bristled. 'I just made a mistake.'

He made many mistakes. As his reputation unravelled we learned that his claim that he had worked without a fee representing the wrongfully deported Vivian Alvarez Solon was a lie. He had charged the Federal Government $72,783.33 for his 'pro bono' work.

The story emerged of the coat 'lost' in New York, for which he had no receipt and for which he allegedly had twice claimed compensation – from the Human Rights Commission, of which he was head, and from his insurance company. He resigned from the HRC soon after.

His claims to have been a director of the famous British chain store Marks & Spencer and of earning degrees, which he had in fact paid for from dubious American universities, were shown to be bogus.

A formal complaint of plagiarism, brought against him in 2003 by Professor John Carter of Sydney University, was revisited. Carter had claimed that Einfeld had used Carter's work without attribution. Einfeld said the footnotes had been lost in the printing process.

Sentencing Einfeld to two years' jail, Justice Bruce James said his offences struck at the heart of the administration of justice. 'Any lawyer, and especially a lawyer who has been a barrister and a judge, who commits such an offence is to be sentenced on the basis that he would have been fully aware of the gravity of his conduct,' he said.

Einfeld's counsel, Ian Barker QC, submitted that Einfeld was a 'beacon of light . . . a living treasure . . . a man of honour'. He said, 'Society owes him a debt, and he's entitled to call it in.' Einfeld later appealed against the sentence on the grounds that he had, unknown to him or anyone else at the time, a long-term bipolar disorder and he was in ill health. He lost the appeal.

Perjury, Justice Einfeld, had said in 2001, sentencing a man, was a most serious offence and deserved significant punishment. 'To tell a deliberate lie or series of lies,' he said, 'regardless of the obligation imposed by an oath to tell the truth . . . is at best arrogant and at worst a complete rejection of law and order and the consensus of the community which alone enables our society to live in freedom and democracy.' He jailed the man for a year.

Marcus Einfeld's clear understanding of the crime of perjury sits uneasily with his muddled understanding of the truth. On *Four Corners* he had this to say on the subject. 'I never lie in statutory declarations if I can conceivably have any hope of it being true. I never tell untruths.'

Well, that was an untruth. Another one.

CAPTAIN MOONLITE's Walk on the Wild Side

Captain Moonlite. It's a name redolent of gallantry, mystery and romantic adventure.

But is there a hint, too, of the love that dared not speak its name; and that in adopting the name Captain Moonlite, the enigmatic bushranger Andrew George Scott was trying to tell us something?

Two young men died in a blaze of gunfire trying to give Scott time to escape. A third went to the gallows with him as Scott stretched out his hand and bade him goodbye. And an hour before he hanged, Scott asked to be buried beside one of the young men who followed him to death.

Blue-eyed, darkly handsome, charming and charismatic, Andrew Scott drew young men, and even boys, to ride with him. Born in Ireland in 1842, the son of an Irish Anglican clergyman, well educated and intelligent, he was a man who had the politician's gift of apparently believing his own lies. Of all the bushrangers, he is the most complex and the only truly enigmatic figure. The truth about Captain Moonlite, like his name, is somewhere in the shadows.

Andrew Scott's life was a kaleidoscope. In turn he was a lay preacher, a bank robber, a notable Sydney socialite, a forger, a convict, a jail-breaker, a lecturer on prison reform, and a bushranger. The central question of his life is what made him lay down the Bible and take up crime. The answer, probably, lies in his disturbed mind. He was an egomaniac who liked to walk on the wild side.

So much of Andrew Scott's life was befuddled by fantasy. He said he fought with Garibaldi in 1859 in Italy's heroic War of Independence, with the Union Army in the American Civil War of 1861–65, and with the British in the bloody Maori Wars of 1861–67, where, he said he was wounded at Waikato. It was true that he limped from wounds in his leg, but if he had fought in three national wars halfway round the world from one another he would hardly have had time to draw breath, let alone immerse himself in engineering, his ostensible occupation, when he came to Melbourne in April 1868.

There, the minister's son soon ingratiated himself with the Anglican bishop. The bishop recommended him to the parish of the Church of the Holy Trinity, Bacchus Marsh, where he took up the position of stipendiary lay reader. His first brush with the law came when he became friends with the son of a wealthy landowner in the district. When the youth was arrested on a charge of cattle duffing, Scott took the stand and provided him with an alibi. The prosecution hinted that Scott himself was involved in the cattle thefts.

The bishop soon after transferred him to the gold-mining town of Mount Egerton, near Ballarat, where it was expected that he would quickly become a minister. Scott was soon one of the community's most valued citizens. Despite his years at war in Italy, the United States and New Zealand, he was clearly a man of peace, a devout Christian. And what a friend he was to so many – particularly the town's young men. With his Irish charm and his adventurous past the young bucks of Mount Egerton saw Scott as a romantic figure. For some, he may have been in more ways than one.

Scott's church was on a hill overlooking the Mount Egerton branch of the London Chartered Bank and it was there, on 8 May 1869, on 'a dark night with a Scotch mist', as bank agent Ludwig Brunn later told a court, 'a man caught hold of me by the left shoulder and said be quiet or I will kill you'. Brunn, an 18-year-old friend of Scott's, was opening the door to the bank when he felt the barrel of a gun between his shoulder blades.

'Andrew!' said young Brunn, recognising his friend's familiar Irish brogue as he was shoved through the open door. Andrew, he saw, was wearing a black cloth mask and a felt hat and waving a pistol. Brunn was chuckling now at the practical joke. 'This is no time for jokes,' the masked man snapped as he held the pistol on Brunn and ordered him to unlock the safe. The masked man stuffed notes, sovereigns, gold flakes and a distinctive, horseshoe-shaped gold bar into a bag and then, limping as Andrew Scott did, he took Brunn across the deserted street to the schoolhouse where another young admirer of his, James Simpson, taught.

He ordered Brunn to sit down with pen and paper and by the light of struck matches he dictated a ludicrous note to the authorities: 'I hereby certify that L.W. Brunn has done everything in his power to withstand our intrusion and the taking away of the money, which was done with firearms.' Scott signed the note, 'Captain Moonlite, Sworn.' He gagged Brunn and tied him to a chair, placed the note on a table beside him, and took his leave. He had got away with cash and gold worth £1195.

Andrew Scott, or Captain Moonlite, either way the man was clearly mentally unbalanced. But the dashing pseudonym served him well. The idea that the god-fearing Andrew Scott might be a bandit by the name of Captain Moonlite was preposterous, and the police brushed aside Brunn's claims that he had indeed been held up by Moonlite and that he was sure Andrew Scott was the man calling himself such. Scott had an alibi, in any case: he had been in Melbourne when the robbery was committed, he said, and he produced a tattered train ticket to prove it. He also intimated that the handwriting on the note might have been the schoolteacher's, James Simpson's.

The police, taking their cue from the lay preacher, charged Brunn and Simpson with the robbery. The charges failed through lack of evidence, but both lost their jobs and their reputations. Devastated, Brunn determined to clear his name.

Scott, for his part, took the advice of the church's authorities and stayed out of the pulpit until things settled down. No doubt realising that Mount Egerton was not where his future lay, he took their suggestion and went to Sydney. With the proceeds of the robbery he quickly established a reputation as a wealthy squatter, a notable new Big Spender in town. He was fast going through the money when he bought a luxury yacht, the *Whynot*. He paid for it, however, with forged credit notes and a bouncing cheque and he was sailing for Fiji with a full crew and had almost cleared the Heads when the police in a steam launch caught up with and arrested him.

Scott was sentenced to 12 months in Maitland jail. He was released in 1872 and found some Victorian police waiting for him outside the gates. They wanted to talk to him about the Mount Egerton bank robbery. Ludwig Brunn had at last got his revenge and cleared the stigma from his name. Brunn had hired a Sydney solicitor, George Sly, to keep a close watch on Scott. Sly was so sympathetic towards Brunn's predicament that he gave his services free and had discovered that the Sydney socialite, widely admired for his dashing style and extravagant lifestyle, had sold a gold bar for £503. Easily recognisable, it was shaped like a horseshoe.

Captain Moonlite was extradited to the newly built Ballarat Gaol. There he was met by a large crowd, eager to see the man who had almost sailed to Fiji in a yacht called *Whynot*. That question, no doubt, reflected the sentiments of some in the crowd. Inside the prison with its 25-foot-high bluestone walls, Scott began at once to plan his escape. In the cell next to him was another Irishman, a man named Dermoodie. Scott cut his way through the wooden partition that separated them, picked the lock with Dermoodie's help and the pair then surprised and overpowered the warder. With his keys they opened the doors of four other cells and released the prisoners. Stripping their beds of blankets, tearing and tying them, the prisoners went to a point of the prison yard where the ground sloped up the walls, formed a human pyramid, and went over by the blanket-rope.

Captain Moonlite was at large once again. He had two weeks of freedom before, one by one, his fellow escapees were caught and he too was found, armed, in a bush hut near Bendigo. He had planned to rob a bank with Dermoodie.

In July 1872, Captain Moonlite, now famous, went up before the feared Judge Redmond Barry. He insisted on conducting his own defence and for a week pleaded his case in a mixture of eloquence and high-flown nonsense that was summed up in his swearing: 'to the God of Heaven, as I pass from this dock to my living tomb, that I am not guilty'. Barry, who did his own line in rhetoric, and liked nothing more than lecturing the wicked before sending them down, gave Captain Moonlite 11 years in Pentridge, Melbourne's new and formidable jail.

He was out in seven and found that Captain Moonlite was no longer news. The newspapers and all the talk was of the Kelly Gang. He missed the limelight. Then he was approached with an invitation to give a series of lectures on prison reform. He was delighted and for a while he was happy: full houses listening to his tales of the wretchedness and wickedness of the prison system. (Scott was an early conspiracy theorist. He claimed that his convictions were the result of The System trying to get him.)

Then interest waned. The Kellys had held up the Bank of New South Wales at Jerilderie and were defying a massive police hunt. The lectures attracted fewer and fewer. Captain Moonlite was yesterday's villain. In Pentridge he had made friends with a 24-year-old robber, James Nesbitt. And in the course of his lectures on the need for prison reform he had met four other feckless young men, all of whom were devoted to him. Thomas Rogan was 23, Graham Bennett, 20, Thomas Williams, 19, and Gus Wernicke, who had met Scott in a Melbourne brothel, just 15. Scott was more than twice his age – 37.

Scott told the gullible young men that he owned a spread at Wagga Wagga, and the six rode from Melbourne for their new life on Captain Moonlite's rural retreat. Only Scott and Nesbitt had handled a gun before, and at least one of the youths, Williams, could barely sit on a horse, but by the time they crossed the Murray and had reached the outskirts of the Wantabadgery Station between Gundagai and Wagga Wagga, they had realised that Scott did not own a property. They'd held up a store and stolen some horses and Scott's band of merry young men were now bushrangers – the Moonliters.

On Friday 14 November 1879, Scott went into the Wantabadgery homestead and asked about work for the six. The manager William Baynes told him there was no work and ordered him to clear off. Scott stormed back to his boys seething with rage.

The next day Captain Moonlite's gang surrounded the homestead and held everyone at gunpoint. For 36 hours the gang terrified more than 30 men, women and children, making wild threats to torture and kill them, holding mock trials and inviting William Baynes to choose the manner of his execution. At one stage Baynes was seated in a buggy, a noose around his neck, when pleading women stopped Scott from whipping the horse forward, using the buggy as the platform drop. Scott's mood was mercurial. When he tried to mount a horse that one of the hostages had ridden in on, it reared, and he shot it in the head. Then he was stricken with remorse.

On Saturday afternoon, unnoticed, Alexander Macdonald, one

of the owners of Wantabadgery, slipped away and went for the Wagga Wagga police, 25 miles away. Four constables rode back with Macdonald and arrived at Wantabadgery at around 4 o'clock on Monday morning to be greeted by a volley of gunfire. Scott and the gang had discovered Macdonald's absence and, alerted by a barking dog, were waiting. The police fell back and retreated to a nearby homestead while one of them rode furiously for Gundagai to get more help.

Their way now clear, the gang rode off late in the morning and along the track encountered and held up a policeman and volunteers on their way to Wantabadgery. They took them with them until they stopped at a slab farmhouse on the slope of a hill owned by Edmund McGlede. They bailed up the McGlede's, told Mrs McGlede to make them breakfast and were just tucking in when a shout came from outside: 'Surrender in the Queen's name!' A bullet shattered the window.

Outside there were 11 policemen and volunteers from Wagga Wagga, Gundagai and Wantabadgery, and around 300 spectators who had walked over the paddocks from Wantabadgery and seated themselves at vantage points on a nearby hill. It was a natural amphitheatre, a precursor to the ultimate reality television show. They enjoyed a thrilling 30 minutes.

The first to die was young Gus Wernicke. Drawing fire from Scott he rushed from the house, darted behind a tree and took aim just as a bullet smashed into his chest. The hillside spectators roared. Wernicke, writhing on the ground, cried, 'Oh God, I'm shot! And I'm only 15!', and a police sergeant fell on him. Bennett, shooting from a window, fell with a wound to his arm.

Then James Nesbitt charged out the front door, his gun blazing. Another cheer went up as he fell dead, shot in the temple by Constable Bowen. In return, Bowen took a fatal bullet in the neck from Captain Moonlite. That left just three of the gang, and when police stormed the house they found Scott and Williams ready to surrender and Rogan, who had not fired a shot, too terrified to come out from under a bed.

Scott was charged with the murder of Bowen and defended himself eloquently on the grounds that he and his gang were retaliating after police opened fire on them. Moreover, he said, a fair trial was impossible because of the publicity he and his co-defendants had been exposed to. The newspapers had condemned him before the trial began, he said. It is a common argument today, but in 1880 it had no chance of succeeding. All four were sentenced to death, but Bennett and Williams, because of their age, had their sentences commuted to life imprisonment.

On the morning of 20 January 1880, at five minutes to nine, Rogan and Scott were led on to the hanging platform at 'Gallows Corner' at Darlinghurst Gaol. The Bulletin's very first issue covered the double hanging and their man described Scott's 'fixed appearance of utter hopelessness and despair. The convict's wasted frame, his sunken eyes, his white face, the helpless, doubled-up appearance . . .'

Captain Moonlite was long gone.

Poor Rogan, the young man who was never meant to be a bushranger, 'simply looked dazed'.

Andrew Scott stretched out his hand to Rogan just before the white cap was placed over his head. 'Goodbye, Tom,' he said and then the trapdoor slammed open.

The Truth About
WILFRED BURCHETT

Media conference, Sydney Airport, 1973:

> REPORTER: Mr Burchett how do you react to statements that people call you a traitor?
> WILFRED BURCHETT: Well my first reaction is to ask them to say that in print and I'll sue them.
> REPORTER: You say you're not a communist, where exactly do you stand politically?
> WILFRED BURCHETT: Where do I stand politically? As a journalist, first of all I'm completely independent, I'm sure it's true to say I'm more independent than anybody in this room.

Independent? That was a lie.
　　Not a communist? That too was a lie. Documents from communist archives in Prague make that clear. And a KGB defector confirmed that Wilfred Burchett was in the pay of the Party.
　　A traitor? Well, that's for you to decide.

An Australian journalist who won international fame for his *Daily Express* report from Hiroshima two weeks after its atomic bombing in 1945. Wilfred Burchett went on to write for the *Times* as its

Eastern Europe correspondent, and for communist newspapers in England and France.

Always he followed the Party line. During the farcical but brutal Stalinist show trials of the fifties he showed no sympathy for those falsely condemned – years later he concluded that the CIA was behind the trials – and for three decades, until his death in 1983 in Bulgaria, he reported from behind enemy lines. His was one of the most influential voices in the anti-American propaganda of the Vietnam War. In the fifties, in Korea, though, Burchett went beyond mere propaganda.

In Pat Burgess's book *Warco: Australian Reporters at War*, Derek Kinne, a British Northumberland Fusilier captured in the Korean War and interned, recounted this meeting with Burchett.

> We'd been in the Chongsam South camp, and were told Wilfred Burchett was going to give us a lecture in the football field...
>
> Burchett said the peace talks had broken down and we were just the lackeys of the Wall Street warmongers. And the more he talked the angrier the people got... Then he really got pissed off and he said, 'OK. So you think that when the Americans come this way you'll be liberated. But I've got news for you, you won't, you'll go that way.' He meant to Manchuria.

Kinne confronted Burchett after the lecture. It was something he was shortly to regret.

> They took me into a room with my hands handcuffed behind my back. They tied a rope around the wrists at the back and pulled it down tight until just my toes were on the ground. Then they started to beat me all over with planks and rifle butts... They put a noose around me neck and the other end in a noose around my leg. So that if I put my leg down, the rope pulled down from the beam and strangled me.

So I said to myself: 'If I'm going to hang, I'm going to hang all at once and not little by little.' So I pulled my leg down real fast, figuring to strangle myself. But they must have been watching because they rushed in and said, 'Confess.' So I said, 'Alright, I confess.'

Editing and reporting to the world the forced 'confessions' of POWs and, particularly American airmen – on the United Nation's alleged use of germ warfare – was what the Chinese paid Burchett to do. So was he a traitor?

In 1986, Robert Manne discussed Burchett on the ABC's *Background Briefing*:

I think it's clear that he was a propagandist for the communist movement... I've made a fairly detailed analysis of his reporting in the Korean War, and there is not a syllable of criticism of the side he supports, not a word of praise for the side that he is against, which is the side of the United Nations, which the Australian forces were supporting.

The second question is whether or not he is an agent or not of the communist side. Now I think there's considerable evidence that he was an agent in the very specific sense that he accepted money for service, and that he was paid and decorated by the communist movement from the 1950s through at least to the 1970s...

The third question is whether or not he was a traitor...he was involved in getting false confessions from American air pilots, and then displaying these confessions to the world as a sign of the guilt of the Americans over germ warfare...

I think he gave more support to the communist side during Korea than any single soldier could have done, even at the highest level, because the pen may not be mightier than the sword, but one pen wielded by someone like Burchett, is much mightier than one sword, and he did very great work with his pen, and with his tape recorder to help in various ways the communist side.

In 1974, Burchett fought an unsuccessful libel case against the Democratic Labor Party Senator Jack Kane. Kane's defence team presented three Australian POWs who said that they had seen Burchett wearing a uniform bearing the insignia of a Chinese colonel. One of the POWs, Thomas Hollis, testified that Burchett urged him, in return for better treatment, to collaborate with Burchett in interrogating POWs. A former US flier also said that he saw Burchett wearing a Chinese colonel's uniform and that Burchett had drafted a 'confession' for him to sign. All told, 30 POWs gave evidence against Burchett. Derek Kinne, the George Cross winner who claimed to have been tortured after confronting Burchett, was among them.

In his autobiography, *Memoirs of a Rebel Journalist: The Autobiography of Wilfred Burchett,* Burchett claimed never to have met Kinne, whom he implies was in the pay of the CIA. 'Once as I was about to enter the courtroom Kinne tried to pull a dramatic stunt by rushing at me and grabbing me around the throat, doing a fairly good imitation of strangling me. But his – or [Dennis] Warner's photographer arrived a fraction too late to achieve the planned effect [of Burchett fighting back and assaulting Kinne].' Burchett wrote that the highly respected journalist Dennis Warner was his 'self-appointed journalistic enemy in Australia, notorious for his close association with the CIA and its Australian equivalent ASIO'.

Burchett had and still has his supporters of course. Harrison Salisbury, the *New York Times* correspondent, saw him as 'a radical who moves through a changing milieu, lending his sympathy to one cause after another, not because of some Marxist doctrine but because he believes in the underdog'. This is hard to square with

Burchett's unwavering support for the Soviet Union, anything but an underdog. Australian journalist John Pilger saw Burchett as a man who had reacted to brutal employers. 'It was against such a background that his radicalism was born; I prefer the word radicalism to socialism, for I believe Wilfred was, above all, a peculiarly Australian radical.'

In 2005, on ABC's *Media Report*, Stephen Crittenden interviewed Burchett's son, George, who had co-edited *Memoirs of a Rebel Journalist: The Autobiography of Wilfred Burchett*.

> STEPHEN CRITTENDEN: What responsibility did you feel . . . testing some of the more controversial issues around your father's story? The germ warfare story in Korea for example, charges that he was involved in interrogating prisoners who'd obviously been tortured?
> GEORGE BURCHETT: . . . all the stuff about KGB and brainwashing is rubbish. Now about what opinions he expressed, that's a separate issue, but as far as I'm concerned truth is sacred, opinions are free, and I don't think anyone ever accused Wilfred of lying or of not telling the truth.

Clearly that wasn't so. Crittenden pushed.

> STEPHEN CRITTENDEN: Well you know, when I read through what he has to say about the trials in Hungary, the show trials in fact of Cardinal Mindszenty and Lazlo Rajk, I'm struck by how kind of casually dismissive he is in his accounts, you know, without a hint of irony he says Cardinal Mindszenty is easy to visualise as an Inquisitor, and yet Cardinal Mindszenty was actually the victim of an inquisition and a show trial on that occasion. The trial of Lazlo Rajk, he says it all sounded incredible, but terribly plausible. And we now know of course

that the Party itself later admitted that the whole thing was a sham, that it was a complete fabrication. Was he really an independent reporter, particularly in that period, or is that actually the biggest fiction about Wilfred Burchett?

In his answer, George Burchett gave a new and novel definition of 'independent' reporting.

> GEORGE BURCHETT: If you ask me, I think he was an independent reporter because he chose to report what he wanted to report. Now how he reported it is of course open to debate. I don't think that the fifties trials is his best expression –
> STEPHEN CRITTENDEN (interrupting): It's not his finest hour.
> GEORGE BURCHETT: No, it is not.

Well, that's something about Wilfred Burchett we can all agree on, then.

When DAISY BATES Met THE BREAKER

She thought he was dashing, a daredevil horseman, handsome, well-spoken and a lover of literature.

And he was.

He thought she was magnetically attractive, feisty, pert, vivacious and well-educated.

And she was.

It may have seemed to them a marriage made in heaven.

In truth it was a marriage made in a back-of-beyond gold-mining town. And in truth they were hiding from each other the same secret: that they were imposters. Edwin Murrant thought his bride Daisy O'Dwyer was an heiress; the blue-blooded daughter of Anglo-Irish landed gentry.

But she wasn't.

Daisy thought her husband Edwin was a young man with great expectations; the illegitimate son of a celebrated admiral of the British Navy.

But he wasn't.

They had sailed from the Old Country to escape lives with little prospect. Both stepped ashore in Queensland in 1883, Daisy aboard the SS *Almora*, at Townsville, and Edwin on the SS *Waroonga*, at

Cooktown. At once they began their double lives.

In the new colony where the European population was centred in just a few outposts they were almost certain to meet, and when they did, bound to be attracted. What no-one could have predicted was the bizarre paths they would follow, Edwin facing a firing squad and Daisy spending most of the remainder of her life dressed in increasingly eccentric antique garb and celebrated throughout the British Empire as the Great White Queen of the Never Never.

The truth about Edwin and Daisy – 'Breaker' Morant and Daisy Bates as they are now known – has only recently emerged. Morant's real identity and background were unearthed shortly after he was executed, in 1902. But Daisy Bates' double life remained her secret until long after her death when historian Susanna de Vries went to Ireland, traced Daisy Bates' beginnings and uncovered the story of Daisy and the Breaker in *Desert Queen: The Many Lives and Loves of Daisy Bates*.

The *Australian Dictionary of Biography* records that Daisy May Bates was 'the daughter of James Edward O'Dwyer, gentleman, and his wife Marguarette, née Hunt'. The *Dictionary* goes on, 'Her mother died in Daisy's infancy and she had an unstable childhood. On the death of her maternal grandmother she was put, aged about 8, in the care of Sir Francis Outram's family in London.'

Not quite. Daisy Dwyer (in her teens she added the O in O'Dwyer) was born poor in County Tipperary, Ireland. Her mother died of tuberculosis when Daisy was four. Her father was a shoemaker who deserted his small children and sailed to Virginia with his second wife, where he died shortly after, an alcoholic. Orphaned, Daisy and her elder sister Kathleen began to invent a life they longed to lead. In their fantasy their father was, Daisy later said, 'the loveliest father in Christendom', a kindly, gentle man who loved her dearly, read Dickens to her, taught her to ride, and to laugh.

She was never in the care of Sir Francis and Lady Outram's

family in London where, she reminisced, 'I became one of the family ... and with them spent happy years in Europe on travel and education ... the gay and dainty Paris of the 1870s ... I shuddered at the dungeons of the Chateau de Chillon ... I ran with terror from hooded monks in the streets of Rome, a smelly city ... we retraced our leisurely way to England through Berlin, Brussels, Antwerp and Ostend ... to Stranorchlar in Scotland near Balmoral Castle. Her Majesty was in residence. The Dowager Lady Outram had taught me how to curtsey and one day I wandered into the castle grounds. Queen Victoria herself was at the moment in the Rose Walk and suddenly appeared. I immediately remembered my manners and dropped the regulation three devout curtseys.'

All beautiful lies. In reality Daisy and her sister Kathleen were briefly raised by their grandmother and educated – very well educated – by nuns at the Convent of the Sacred Heart until Kathleen was 20 and Daisy 19, both working as pupil-teachers. When they left the convent they had command of French and German; their Irish accent had been softened to a charming burr beneath an English upper-class accent. They were ideally suited to be governesses, educating the children of the well-to-do and – with luck – making an advantageous marriage from the sons of their employees.

Kathleen did just that, marrying the son of a wealthy English Protestant family. (By this time the young women had put their Catholic past behind them.) And Daisy seemed set to follow in her footsteps with Ernest Baglehole, the son of a ship and factory owner, when Ernest's parents demanded he marry another. He did as ordered, in 1881. Ernest's wedding photograph shows a man with the face of a well-tended grave. This may have been partly to do with his surname, but, as he made clear a few years later, he was also rueing the loss of Daisy. As Daisy was rueing his loss.

Frustrated, she set sail for Australia, hoping, perhaps, to meet a black sheep English aristocrat who had dug up a very large nugget in the goldfields or a kindly cattle king who would read Dickens to her after the servants retired.

Instead, she met a young American journalist, Arnold Colquhoun. Arnold was exotic, volatile, besotted, but unstable, and when Daisy found he was also syphilitic, unsuitable. When she told him this, Colquhoun took a fatal cocktail of morphine and alcohol. Daisy left town and took a position as governess on Fanning Downs Cattle Station outside Charters Towers where she met a young jackaroo, Edwin 'Henry' Murrant.

Murrant was the son of a Somerset workhouse keeper and matron. He had won a scholarship to an elite private school and, like Daisy, he had stayed on to be a pupil-teacher. There he learned the manners and the mores of an English upper-class gentleman, writing verse, riding to hounds, honing his accent and boasting of his 'Guv'nor', Admiral Sir George Digby Morant of Bideford, Devon.

Admiral Morant, Edwin insisted, was his real father. Daisy, perhaps scenting that there was money to be had, persuaded Edwin to change his name to Morant. The station hands, in admiration of his expertise at breaking horses, had already nicknamed him 'the Breaker' and he became known, in time, as Harry 'the Breaker' Morant.

Daisy and Edwin wed in 1884, shortly after they met, both falsifying their ages. Daisy said she was 21, three years younger than she was, and Edwin added two years to his age, also claiming to be 21. Hardly had they settled into the bliss of married life than a Charters Towers jeweller knocked on the door of their humble cottage, demanding payment for the wedding ring – Edwin's cheque had bounced. His cheques were bouncing all over Queensland. Next came the Anglican Minister who had officiated at the wedding, asking in vain for his small fee. And finally, the police, investigating an allegation of a woman friend of Edwin's from whom he had stolen a saddle and some pigs.

Edwin no doubt felt claustrophobic; to get away from it all, he galloped out of town. Constable Quinn gave chase, caught up with him and brought him back in handcuffs. The magistrate found there was insufficient evidence to convict. Not so Daisy. The two, possibly by mutual consent, never again met or spoke of the marriage.

Edwin went on work as an itinerant drover, a bar brawler, a bad poet writing under the *nom de plume* 'the Breaker' and a superb horseman who allegedly rode with a copy of Byron's poetry in his pack. Inevitably, he drifted to Sydney. There, as Breaker Morant, he wrote his doggerel bush ballads for the *Bulletin* and drank with the likes of Henry Lawson and 'Banjo' Paterson before finding himself fighting for the Empire against the Boers in South Africa.

Daisy meanwhile wasted no time in remarrying, bigamously. Eleven months after she wed Edwin Murrant she promised to love, honour and obey Jack Bates, a tall, handsome drover. Daisy met Jack at the Bates' home near Nowra, New South Wales, where she had taken a job as governess to a widow, Catherine Bates', the mother of six small children.

Jack arrived home on Christmas Eve and Daisy was immediately drawn to him. Like Murrant, Bates was a fine horseman, but he was also the strong silent type who had no use for books and who Daisy should have realised was never going to be part of her plans. She should have realised too, that Bates would never become a station master, as Daisy would have liked, and that instead life as a drover's wife would be long and lonely.

Jack rushed Daisy off her feet. And Jack was head over heels in love. In these unstable positions they were both vulnerable. Three days after they first met he proposed. And one February morning, eight weeks after they met, he invited her to ride with him to look at an old Anglican church. When they got there and entered the church the minister was waiting and Daisy found herself married in her riding dress. Their marriage certificate records that Daisy was a 21-year-old spinster. (She was still married to Murrant and never did divorce him.) Almost immediately after the wedding Jack went droving.

Four months later she married again.

This time the groom was Ernest Baglehole, the same Baglehole who had dashed her hopes in England by marrying. Now, four years later, he was in Australia and in touch with her. Of all the veils Daisy drew over her life, her third marriage in two years is the most impenetrable. We know that Daisy invented an excuse to her mother-in-law, saying she needed to go to Sydney to shop for household goods and that on 10 June 1885 she married Ernest Baglehole.

Once again, bride and groom falsified their ages, Daisy still claimed to be a 21-year-old spinster, and Ernest claimed to be a bachelor. Not long after, husband number three left Sydney, never to be heard of again. Why and when he left or where he went and what happened to him, we don't know. Daisy took care to obliterate all letters, photographs and records relating to her marriages to Murrant and Baglehole. What she couldn't conceal was her pregnancy: on 26 August 1886, to her great irritation, she gave birth to an unwanted boy, Arnold Hamilton Bates.

Jack Bates had come back from droving 12 months before and it is possible that he was Arnold's father. It is equally possible that the baby was Ernest Baglehole's. It's possible, too, that Jack met the Breaker, who was also droving at the time, and that they shared a beer or fell to fighting – things they both enjoyed – in a bar somewhere back of Bourke. Daisy Bates' labyrinthine life was already much stranger than fiction.

Daisy left Jack and Arnold and went back to England, her marriage to Jack seemingly over. She found office work with the great journalist William Stead and enjoyed a busy social life. Her biographer Susanna de Vries speculates that she may have been 'some kind of high-class call girl at weekend house parties', like another member of Stead's office staff, a woman Daisy described as an 'elegant, aristocratic and frail young creature' who bed-hopped at country house weekend parties.

What is certain is that she had affairs. 'Men loved Daisy too much,' her sister-in-law Mrs Charlie Bates said. It's reasonable to conclude that some of them were with wealthy married men. 'I like to fall in love, just meet and then part. Life was fun that way,' Daisy told a London journalist years later.

Then came a letter from Jack. He wanted her to come home; he planned to buy a property in Western Australia. Astonishingly, Daisy agreed. After five years in London she was set to sail once again to Australia when the *Times* published a letter about atrocities suffered by Western Australian Aborigines under white settlers. Daisy proposed to the *Times* that she would report on the situation and the paper agreed.

It was the beginning of more than 35 years living with, studying, feeding, clothing and caring for Aborigines in Western and South Australia, dressed all the while in archaic Victorian clothing, ankle-length skirts, high-neck blouses, boots, gloves and a veil under sailor hats, and supplemented at times by pistols at her waist.

Daisy became Daisy Bates CBE, an outstanding eccentric revered by the Aboriginal people she worked with and admired throughout the Empire. She was also a respected anthropologist, though not by most in her profession. They did not share her repeated contention that Aborigines practised cannibalism: 'There is not one child [at Ooldea in South Australia, where Daisy worked] who has not eaten [a] portion of his brother or sister . . . all the natives in the area . . . are cannibals.'

By 1902 Daisy had finally separated from two of her husbands, Jack Bates and Breaker Morant, the latter terminally separated just before dawn on 25 February when Morant looked down the 18 gun barrels levelled at him by a detachment of Cameron Highlanders and barked, 'Shoot straight you bastards! Don't make a mess of it!'

Or perhaps not. Breaker Morant's defiant last words are in dispute, as is the truth about his reasons for shooting unarmed prisoners. Morant and his fellow-Australian PJ Handcock faced the firing squad after being found guilty of murder. But was it murder or were they following orders?

The pair had come to South Africa in 1900, along with 16,000 other Australians, to fight for Britain in the Second Boer War – the British Empire against the Boer inhabitants of two Dutch South African republics: the Transvaal Republic and the Orange Free State. Morant and Handcock joined the Bushveldt Carbineers, an irregular unit fighting a brutal guerrilla war in which both sides committed atrocities. The Boers sometimes wore British khaki uniforms to deceive, had no respect for the white flag of surrender and dynamited trains. The British commander-in-chief General Kitchener's response to the train-wrecking was to order the placement of Boer women and children in the front carriages of trains. He also established the first concentration camps, where tens of thousands died. He also issued orders – verbal orders – to 'take no prisoners'.

The Carbineers had shot several prisoners before Morant arrived and when Captain Percy Hunt, his best mate and superior officer, reprimanded him for bringing in prisoners, Morant took no notice. Then Hunt led an unsuccessful attack on a farmhouse and was wounded and left behind during the action. They next day they found his naked body, battered and mutilated. Morant set out for revenge. His patrol captured a Boer whom Morant believed was using Hunt's trousers as a pillow (though they were later found to be of a much older origin) and Morant ordered him shot. Three other officers had apparently decided they would follow orders: they would shoot all Boer prisoners.

Other killings followed. On 23 August 1901, Morant led a patrol to intercept a group of eight prisoners who were being brought in for questioning. Morant ordered them to be taken to the side of the road and shot. A South African–born German missionary spoke to the Boers before their execution. Morant later shot dead the padre as he was on his way to report the murders to the British authorities. Morant said later that he believed the padre to be a spy. Kitchener had the Bushveldt Carbineers officers arrested.

'He had always been the underdog,' 'Banjo' Paterson wrote in the *Bulletin*, 'and now he was up in the stirrups it went to his head like wine.' Paterson's assessment of incidents half a world away may have been a little subjective. Morant himself wanted people to know his side of the story, that he had been acting under the army's direction, '. . . see the *Bulletin* people in Sydney town and tell 'em all the facts,' he wrote to a friend. The court martial, meanwhile, heard all the facts over five weeks, and sentenced Moran and Handcock to death. A third Australian, Whitton, got life imprisonment and was freed within three years.

Was the sentence just? Geoffrey Robertson, Australia's noted barrister and human rights advocate, gave Nick Bleszynski, author of *Shoot Straight You Bastards,* this legal opinion: 'Morant's trial was a particularly pernicious example of using legal proceedings against lower ranks as a means of covering up the guilt of senior officers and of Kitchener himself, who gave or approved their unlawful "shoot to kill" order. Morant may have been all too happy to obey it, of course, in which case he deserved some punishment. But it was wrong to use him as a scapegoat for an unlawful policy. I regard the convictions of Morant and Handcock as unsafe.'

The executions shocked Australians, and Breaker Morant was mourned, soon to become a near-mythical figure. This annoyed the historian Manning Clark, who thundered, 'Once again Australia and its savage past caused its victims to celebrate as a folk hero a liar, a thief and a drunken lout, a scoundrel, a believer in the rule of fist and a murderer of innocent people.'

Perhaps none mourned more than Daisy Bates. She surely shed a tear for the Breaker.

But then, with Daisy Bates, you could be sure of nothing.

STORM's Scandal and CARLTON's Blue

David Gallop, the National Rugby League's astute chief executive, must have nodded off some nights dreaming of League dominating the media in Melbourne. League leading the TV news, League on the front pages, League on the back pages. League the talk of talk show radio. League the buzz over a million Melbourne café lattes. Rugby League sweeping Australian Football off the radar.

Well, it happened. It was no dream. But it *was* a nightmare.

When David Gallop woke on 23 April 2010, the Melbourne *Age* front page carried the 120-point splash: 'Stripped of everything' and above it an eight-column pointer: 'SPORTS' BIGGEST SCANDAL. Special report: Inside the demise of Melbourne Storm'.

The *Herald Sun* gave the news its front page, its back page and page after page and thousands of column centimetres in between. The Storm dominated radio talk shows, led the TV news bulletins and captured AFL TV shows. Rugby League *was* the talk of the town. It was the talk of the nation.

As media coverage went it was the perfect storm. It was just not the one that David Gallop had dreamed of.

The story broke quickly. It began with a whistleblower who

alerted the NRL to the Storm's salary-cap scam. As a result, auditors visited the Storm headquarters at Princes Park, Carlton, the home of the Carlton Football Club, itself the centre of a 2002 salary cap rort. There they were shown perfectly legitimate account books. Then one of the Storm staffers innocently opened a door to a room where the investigators stumbled on another set of accounts, books that revealed the club had been systematically exceeding its salary cap for the past five years. In four of those past five years the Storm had played in a Grand Final.

The second, covert books, showed how Melbourne Storm, voted the Team of the Decade, had gained its extraordinary success. In 10 years the club had made the Grand Final five times and won three times, had won two World Cup Challenges and could boast three successive Golden Boot Awards (for the world's best player).

The Rugby League team established in 1998 in the heartland of Australian Football was clearly the best of the modern era and, some thought, the finest of all time. The Storm, coached by wily hardhead Craig Bellamy, had the most dazzling stars in the competition: Cameron Smith, an outstanding captain; Billy Slater, arrogantly, brazenly brilliant; Cooper Cronk, a Dally M Halfback of the Year; and Greg Inglis, dynamic and destructive, perhaps the best of them all, winner of a Golden Boot, a Dally M representative Player of the Year, a Dally M Halfback of the Year and a Rugby League International Federation Centre of the Year.

The Storm was the favourite for the 2010 Premiership and in two weeks the players were due to play their first game at their new home in the country's newest football venue, the state-of-the-art 'bubble wrap' AAMI stadium. Then the NRL investigator flipped on the light in that backroom. David Gallop summarily stripped Melbourne Storm of the two premierships it had won during its dual books years and banned it from winning competition points in 2010. The NRL also fined the club a staggering $1.7 million.

It was the harshest penalty ever given to an Australian football club and, the columnists, shock jocks and editorial writers agreed, a sporting scandal the like of which we'd never seen. Many called for an end to Melbourne Storm.

Gerard Whateley, the Melbourne commentator for ABC *Grandstand* wrote:

> For the sporting public of Melbourne it's personal. For these are people who have been taken advantage of in the most cynical manner. Because the fraud is one thing. The betrayal quite another.
>
> The Storm wooed a city with fine players who were granted a place in many hearts despite playing a code diametrically opposed to our sensibility.
>
> Their place was at the fringe of the mainstream and we shouldn't pretend otherwise. But the goodwill was real. The Storm carried the Melbourne name and that entitled them to support and in turn brought pride.
>
> Their ability to upset those in Sydney was among their most endearing qualities. Something we could all understand.
>
> It was a lie. A cruel deception.

Two weeks prior to the scandal, Sydney journalist Malcolm Knox wrote, presciently:

> Handled correctly, the NRL's salary cap investigation into Cameron Smith can solve fifteen-sixteenths of the code's problems as it heads toward an independent commission. All it needs to do is recommend that Smith's club, the Melbourne Storm, be wound up.
>
> The Storm, like Paterson's Curse, is a pretty-looking purple noxious weed. A very well-run and successful rugby league club, with three premierships in its first decade and a bit, a brilliant coach and some of the best players in the game's history,

Melbourne is the extravagant indulgence that is dragging everything else down.

So, we were all on the same front page. Melbourne Storm was a disgrace. 'Shut the door. Turn out the lights. Never return. It's time to leave Melbourne Storm. You're not welcome any more. Not ever again,' as Whateley lamented.

But was the Storm the sole salary-cap sinner? Chris Anderson, the club's first coach told the *Age* that he believed the other 15 clubs had probably cheated. 'Everyone has had a shot at the salary cap,' he said. 'I don't think the other clubs have been completely blameless over the years. I think the other clubs are just as culpable.'

Melbourne Storm former CEO Brian Waldron would agree. The man who was at the centre of scandal, when asked by the club's chairman Rod Moodie why he had breached the code, replied, 'Because everyone does.'

That may have been true of the NRL. But it's unlikely to be so in the AFL. Not after the way Carlton was dealt with in 2002, when the club was found to have rorted the salary cap over four years, fined $987,500 and, most punishingly for a club on the bottom of the ladder, banned from the first two rounds of the national draft for two years.

Carlton, established in 1864, and, with Essendon, the most successful team in the AFL, 'won' its first Wooden Spoon that year, 2002, finishing last as it did again in 2005 and 2006. It had taken more than a century to get those spoons and the wrath of the Carlton faithful was ferocious. The club president, 'Big Jack' Elliott, fell on his sword and resigned. That wasn't enough for the Blues. His name, honoured on the club's main grandstand, the John Elliott Stand, was taken down; removed forever from sight like some disgraced pharaoh.

John Elliott could have been, many thought, prime minister.

Others believed he could have been Bozo the Clown. In the eighties, Elliot was an immensely wealthy and successful businessman – President of the Liberal Party, Chairman and Chief Executive of Elders IXL and sitting in the boardrooms of BHP and National Mutual. Elliott delivered Carlton a premiership and was seen as a knockabout, if abrasive, bloke who happened to be wallowing in money. In the nineties came another premiership, but his commercial activities were beginning to shake his once-indomitable optimism and eat into his $80 million fortune.

In 2005, when the AFL's denial of Carlton's top draft picks hit the fans, Elliott was in disgrace. At the same time he was fighting legal battles against the National Crime Authority and the Australian Securities and Investments Commission, the collapse of his rice milling business and bankruptcy. His personal life, too, was in turmoil. Worst of all, for Carlton fans, he once sent the team out to play not in the 'Old Dark Navy Blue' they had worn for a century and half, but in baby blue, promoting Smarties. The horror, the horror.

'Big Jack' hit the bottom in 2009 when he was told he was no longer welcome at Carlton after he publicly reminisced at the 7th annual Ron Barassi Senior Memorial Debate in Hobart:

> When I was at Carlton in my 20 years . . . I think we had people who claimed to be raped by our players – women they were – not men – on four or five occasions. Not once did any of these stories get into the press because in those days they probably only had 20 people writing in the press and they weren't interested in all that sort of nonsense. We'd pay the sheilas off and wouldn't hear another word.

'Big Jack' heard many another word after that. None more quirky and candid than Sam Newman's on Nine's *The Footy Show*.

'Nature had made him a slave and an idolater,' said Newman,

quoting a 19th-century English poet, much to the perplexity of the viewing audience. 'His mind resembles those creepers which the botanists call parasites, and which can subsist only by clinging round the stems and imbibing the juices of stronger plants.'

Newman, perhaps realising that this metaphor was too horticultural for some, came down to earth: 'Jack, if you're listening you are a stupid, selective pariah and you want to wake up to yourself. You've just set that club back and all their great work. It's just about you . . . you've got your head up your arse, mate.'

And they say it's only a game.

PETER FOSTER and the Riddle of His Underpants Escape

The international media almost invariably prefixes Peter Foster's name with the words 'confidence man'.

Peter Foster himself prefers to be known as his website bills him: International Man of Mischief.

But for millions of men Peter Foster is the International Man of Mystery. They want to know how on earth he managed to bed the page-three topless totty Samantha Fox? Samantha's spectacular assets made Peter Foster famous. If not for them, Foster would be just another dodgy salesman, the sort we see each weeknight extending a puffy palm to the lens of *Today Tonight*'s camera while squeezing into his getaway BMW. But Samantha Fox put Foster on the front pages and it's a position that, you suspect, he likes.

After Samantha he again made the splash stories internationally acting as financial advisor for Cherie Blair, the wife of the then UK Prime Minister Tony Blair. The result was the Cheriegate scandal in which Mrs Blair was accused of improper land dealings. She claimed that Foster was not involved but later, tearfully, had to admit that she had sent Foster an email in which she said, 'We are on the same wavelength, Peter.' Foster's then lover Carole Caplin was a close confidante of Cherie and at one time the Blairs had agreed to be godparents to her child. Carole miscarried and Foster later alleged that Tony Blair had made Carole pregnant.

We all know a Peter Foster. There's one like him in every school. The rascal who can be relied on to break the rules – all of them; the cocky, slippery kid who take the short cut and gets away with it; the back-of-the-class, plain boy – and let's be fair, Peter Foster is unprepossessing – who somehow, maddeningly, seems to be always surrounded by girls.

Some of these likely lads leave school early and carve a career selling insurance or used cars or, like Peter Foster, slimming aids. Others graduate and become business tycoons or lawyers. Peter Foster went to school on the Gold Coast, a sunny place for shady people, and as a 14-year-old was leasing pinball machines, earning him considerably more than his teachers' incomes. At 15, school behind him, he was promoting theme nights at a disco and at 17 he promoted an elimination world title fight between two genuine title contenders, Britain's light heavyweight champion Bunny Johnson and Australia's Tony Mundine, the introvert father of the extrovert Anthony 'the Man' Mundine.

Penthouse called Peter Foster, in those Gold Coast days, 'Kid Tycoon'. He had confidence but more, he had chutzpah, that supercharged audacity best defined by the boy who murdered his parents and then pleaded for sympathy because he was an orphan. Judging a beauty contest at a Surfers Paradise disco, the teenage Foster is said to have gone backstage and asked the contestants: 'OK, which one of you wants to put this beyond doubt?'

In 1983, aged 21, Foster was staying with Muhammad Ali and Ali's third wife Veronica at their Los Angeles home. He was producing a television documentary on the great boxer. That was a coup but what he found on the kitchen bench of the Ali home was to make him a multimillionaire by his mid-twenties.

Veronica Ali, a model, drank a Chinese tea, Bai Lin, believing it helped control her weight. Foster saw an opportunity. He bought the rights for Bai Lin Tea in Australia, marketed it as a slimming aid, and watched it take off. He moved into international markets – South Africa, England and Europe. Bai Lin's remarkable properties were sworn to by Lester Piggott, the legendary English jockey; Fergie, the 'Duchess of Pork', then the Queen's daughter-in-law; and the equally famous and bountiful page-three poppet Samantha Fox.

Peter Foster was, surely, a happy man. He was dating Samantha, the Bai Lin Tea logo was on the blue jersey of the Chelsea Football Club and all was right with the world. Suddenly it all went wrong. The problem was that Bai Lin was not a magic potion that caused the kilos to drop off. It was simply tea. That revelation led Foster on a labyrinthine path of convictions, imprisonment and escapes from imprisonment that was summed up as early as 2003 in a civil case brought by the Australian Competition and Consumer Commission. Justice Spender had this to say about Peter Foster [transcript edited]:

- Mr Foster has had a sad and lengthy history of dishonesty, deception and evasion.
- There is evidence suggesting that Mr Foster was prepared to manufacture evidence for the purpose of obtaining necessary visas for residing in Fiji.
- I made Mr Foster bankrupt on 26 November 1984. Mr Foster denied in public examinations on 18 April 1985 and on 12 and 13 March 1987 that he was involved in the management of Slimway Tea Co Pty Ltd. On 1 October 1987, Mr Foster pleaded guilty to a charge that whilst an insolvent under administration, he took part in the management of Slimway Tea Co Pty Ltd.

- In June 1988, a warrant for Mr Foster's arrest and that of his mother was issued in the United Kingdom for their failure to appear on charges concerning contravention of the *UK Trade Descriptions Act* involving a company called Slimweight Co UK Ltd.
- On 5 January 1989, Mr Foster requested his passport from his Trustee and gave an undertaking that he would travel to Taipei and the United Kingdom only. Mr Foster departed Australia on 22 February 1989 and sent letters to the Official Receiver dated 21 and 30 March 1989 purportedly from Solihull in the United Kingdom. However, at that time Mr Foster was in California.
- On 5 July 1989, he was charged in the United States with offences relating to false advertising and the advertising of drugs. On 7 July 1989, he pleaded no contest to three of seven counts and was convicted accordingly. He was ordered, amongst other things, to perform 90 days community service and pay restitution of US$228,000 and investigation costs of US$10,000 before 16 March 1990. He was in prison until 23 August 1989. On that day he was released from prison and taken into custody by US immigration authorities. He was [granted] bail on 24 August 1989 to appear on 3 October 1989 to show cause [as to] why he should not be excluded from the United States of America. The United States City Attorney retained Mr Foster's passport.
- On 28 August 1989, Mr Foster replied for a replacement passport at the Australian Consulate in Los Angeles ... the claim was made that the original had been lost. A replacement passport was issued. Mr Foster, before me, swore that the consular official was told of the fact that the Los Angeles authorities had Mr Foster's passport and Mr Foster was directed to fill in the document with the false

declaration in it. This explanation is incredible.
- On 7 September 1989, Mr Foster left the United States and returned to Australia. He did not perform his community service or make the orders, restitution or pay the investigation costs ordered, and he did not attend the immigration hearing scheduled for 3 October 1989. A warrant was issued for his arrest in Los Angeles on 16 March 1990.
- In the course of Mr Foster's proceedings in California, a letter from Mr Foster was sent to his accountant in the United Kingdom dated 21 March 1989. That letter said, in part: '. . . so they don't know where I am, I have said they can communicate with me through my accountant in England, therefore, you may get a fax for me care of your office. If you do, can you just direct it on to me here – they do not know I am in America and I certainly don't want them to find out. I am due to be discharged in November so I only have to stall for a few more months.'
- In July 1989, the Official Receiver in Australia became aware from United Kingdom authorities that Mr Foster had never in fact returned to the United Kingdom as he purported to do.
- I believe that there is a strong chance that Mr Foster will not remain in the jurisdiction, or return to it, to contest the allegations made against him by the ACCC [Australian Competition and Consumer Commission].

Oh, what a tangled web. But of course it didn't end there.

In 2007, Andrew Denton interviewed Foster on *Enough Rope*. It was Foster's second appearance on the show. Denton began:

> Interviewing white collar criminals is probably the toughest part of this job. They're harder to talk to than politicians because

lying isn't just a habit for them, it's a business practice. If they can they'll try to play you like they play everybody, with a carefully marked deck. The trick is, to recognise the cards.

Tonight's main guest Peter Foster is ultimately in the business of selling himself. He bought the full deck of cards marked 'trust me' to our studio. Before getting to Foster's interview, and the off-screen drama that followed, let's remind ourselves of what has been happening in Peter's life since we chatted in 2004. He was last seen at Brisbane airport in February being arrested for money laundering.

The charge related to an alleged fraud in which it is claimed Foster convinced a Fijian bank to give him $700,000 to build a resort on land he didn't own. Foster arrived in Brisbane fresh from a Vanuatu jail, locked up after fleeing charges in Fiji of forgery and falsifying his criminal history to gain a work permit. It was in that country that Foster suffered the indignity of being arrested in his underpants while making a bold swim for freedom.

The mystery of Peter Foster is not that he squired Samantha Fox for a number of years. (The secret, he told Denton, was the reverse-sell: he played hard to get). No, the real mystery is why he spent half his lifetime and his considerable talent to get to the point where he was arrested in his underpants while making a bold swim for freedom.

THE HOAXES

Something that
has been established
or accepted by
fraudulent means

The Imagination of
FRANK HARDY

Frank Hardy died at his desk with a form guide in his hand in January 1994. He was 76. It seemed apposite, somehow.

Hardy liked to portray himself as a battler from the bush, a self-educated man who had to leave home at 13 'because my dad couldn't get the dole with me at home'. The Hardy family was twice evicted during the Depression, he said, and to find jobs his father Tom had to move from place to place, working in milk factories. He himself had struggled to survive as a youth, labouring in a Bacchus Marsh milk factory, digging potatoes and picking tomatoes and fruit.

Frank's brother Jim had different memories. 'We were never evicted from any house we lived in,' he told the Melbourne *Herald*. 'My brother did not leave home so my father could get the dole. There was no reason. Our father never lost a day's work in his working life. He worked for only two companies [as a dairy inspector] . . . over a period of 34 years. Father retired in 1942 due to illness. He died of cancer in 1943, in his fifties.'

An imaginative man, Frank was one of eight highly talented children in the Hardy family. His brother Jim was a songwriter and a professional entertainer. His vivacious and quick-witted sister Mary Hardy won seven TV Logies and his pigtailed granddaughter

Marieke is a provocative writer. Frank came out of the Depression and went to Melbourne to work for the *Radio Times* as a cartoonist (he'd done a commercial art course by correspondence) and advertising salesman. He married Rosslyn Cooper in 1940 in Melbourne's St Patrick's Cathedral, and later that year joined the Australian Communist Party.

In 1942 he was called up and spent the rest of the war in the army, stationed in the Northern Territory. There he turned his hand to poetry and anecdotes for his unit's *Troppo Tribune,* and for the Australian Imperial Force magazine *Salt*. Two of his short stories won competitions and soon his work was being accepted by *Coast to Coast* and the *Guardian.*

After the war, Hardy worked part-time as a journalist and began researching his first novel *Power Without Glory*. At the heart of *Power Without Glory* is John West, the sinister political manipulator and racketeer. He is clearly meant to be seen as the prominent Melbourne millionaire, John Wren. The Communist Party conceived a plan to attack Wren and his associates as a way of undermining the Party's trade union rivals from the Catholic-based Movement – the Industrial Groupers – as well as the Labor Party and capitalism.

Hardy was charged with criminal libel, on the depiction in his novel that 'John West's' wife was having an affair. Wren had little option. Had he invoked criminal charges on the basis that he was West, he would have been open to cross-examination on the many activities that West was involved in. There is no doubt that Wren had been involved in some dubious doings, and that he was a power broker in the Labor Party politically, but essentially he was a hugely successful illegal bookmaker who became an entrepreneur. Wren, along with Hugh D McIntosh, was one of Australia's foremost promoters of public entertainment of the first half of the 20th century. He was also a noted philanthropist and the uncrowned emperor of the Collingwood Football Club.

In her book *Frank Hardy and the Making of Power Without Glory,* Pauline Armstrong establishes that there were no reasonable foundations on which Hardy could base the incident of Mrs West's adultery. Hardy himself, late in his life, admitted to having doubts about the alleged affair and wrote another novel, he said, because of a 'deep inner need to express regret about the so-called adultery allegations'. But some parts of *Power Without Glory* were based on true incidents and others rang true when they were aired in court, and it was difficult to separate fact from fiction.

In 1992, one of Hardy's barristers, the future Supreme Court justice Sir John Starke, in an extraordinary revelation, admitted that the defence team used this confusion to sling as much mud as possible so that at least some would stick. This so incensed Wren that he proposed challenging Don Campbell KC, Hardy's defence counsel, to a duel.

In a letter to Campbell, Wren said that the only course available to him to defend his wife's honour was to challenge him to a duel with fists or revolver – 'the former preferred'. Wren's son John said he persuaded his father not to send the letter because it would have caused further anguish to Mrs Wren. (In any case it couldn't have been fisticuffs, it would have had to have been pistols and Zimmer frames at dawn – Wren was 79 at the time and could hardly walk and Campbell wore leg callipers and walked with sticks.)

The libel case riveted Australia. The committal proceedings 'were front-page news all over Australia,' Starke said. 'Campbell got in, one way or another, every piece of roguery we could lay our hands on, and there was plenty of it, against old man Wren, and it was published in all the papers.'

Campbell was just as ruthless with his client. Starke revealed that Campbell told Hardy, '"My fees and Jack Starke's fees [two hundred pounds a day] are to be paid to our clerk at 10 o'clock each morning of the trial." Hardy looked a bit taken aback. He said, "And what will happen if they're not, Mr Campbell?" "Oh," he said, "don't you worry, Hardy, don't you worry at all. On that day Starkey and I won't be appearing for you." The fees were paid at 10 o'clock every morning, I can tell you.'

Campbell argued that the case was not a matter of truth or falsity, but whether Hardy referred to real or fictional characters. But even if identification was intended, he said, the book depicted 'a good moral and religious woman driven to adultery by the nefarious conduct of her husband, and therefore she is not to be looked down upon'.

The jury took just one hour to return a not-guilty verdict. The book, the jury decided, was fiction.

Campbell and Starke had expected Hardy would get five years. Hardy himself admitted that he should have been found guilty – he had publicly represented his novel to be based on fact, but the law deemed it to be fiction, and the jury, it's said, didn't like what they'd heard about Wren. A few years later, Starke met the jury foreman at the races. He told Starke that the jury had no sympathy for Wren: 'He'd been a scandal all his life, and the first time he's hurt by anything he rushes to the law.'

From 1954, Frank and Rosslyn Hardy and their three children made their home in Sydney. Frank's court case and his triumphant acquittal had made him a national figure, reckoned by many to be a heroic, literary giant. In 1952, he went to Russia and wrote *Journey Into the Future,* praising the USSR and Joseph Stalin, the 'only dishonest book' he said he ever wrote, and the following year stood as a senate candidate for Victoria. He was unsuccessful, as he was in 1955 standing for a seat in the House of Representatives. In 1955 and again in 1967 he was rejected for a position on the National Committee of the Communist Party of Australia.

Hardy became known as a television and radio panellist, book reviewer and playwright, and in the late 1960s campaigned for land rights for the Gurindji, two of whom came to his funeral, along with Gough Whitlam and other prominent Labor Party figures.

Mick Eangiari of the Gurindji remembered that Hardy 'sat in the dust with us fellas. He had a yarn and he put our true words in a book about the Vestey mob. He was a really true man.'

Up to a point, Mr Eangiari.

ERN MALLEY Turns on His Frankensteins

'You are my creator, but I am your master – obey!'
— The Monster, *Frankenstein*, Mary Shelley

It seemed like a brilliant idea at the time. And it was. For a time. One Saturday afternoon in October 1943, in Melbourne's bluestone Victoria Barracks, the headquarters of the Australian Army, Lieutenant James McAuley and Corporal Harold Stewart began writing the literary fraud of the century.

Both men were poets of considerable talent, irked by the modernist school of poetry where clarity and construction were spurned in favour of the surreal and the opaque. They were particularly irritated by the Adelaide poet, Max Harris, a few years younger than them, the editor of *Angry Penguins*, a journal of poetry, art and commentary that was defiantly modernist.

McAuley and Stewart had similar backgrounds. Both came from the battling class of the western suburbs of Sydney. Both were gifted musicians and brilliant writers. Stewart once sat an English exam in which he declined to answer all but one question: the meaning of the word irony. His answer ran to 30 foolscap pages. Both went to Sydney's famous Fort Street High School. McAuley was school captain. And he and Stewart edited the school paper, the *Fortian*.

Both went on to Sydney University where they cemented their friendship and when war came, both found themselves at the nerve centre of Australia's military, the Victoria Barracks.

It was there, that October Saturday afternoon, that they created Ern Malley. McAuley and Stewart later wrote in a joint-statement to Sydney newspaper *Fact* on 25 June 1944:

> We decided to carry out a serious literary experiment...
>
> For some years now we have observed with distaste the gradual decay of meaning and craftsmanship in poetry.
>
> Mr Max Harris and other *Angry Penguin* writers represent an Australian outcrop of a literary fashion which prominent in England and America. The distinctive features of the fashion, it seemed to us, was that it renders its devotees insensible of absurdity and incapable of ordinary discrimination.
>
> Our feeling was that by a process of critical self-delusion and mutual admiration, the perpetrators of this humorless nonsense had managed to pass it off to would be intellectuals and Bohemians, here and abroad, as great poetry.
>
> Their work appeared to us to be a collection of garish images without coherent meaning and structure; as if one erected a coat of bright paint and called it a house.
>
> However, it was possible that we had simply failed to penetrate to the inward substance of these productions. The only way of settling the matter was by experiment. It was, after all, fair enough. If Mr Harris proved to have sufficient discrimination to reject the poems, then the tables would have been turned.
>
> What we wished to find out was: Can those who write, and those who praise so lavishly, this kind of writing tell the real product from consciously and deliberately concocted nonsense?
>
> We gave birth to Ern Malley. We represented Ern though

his equally fictitious sister Ethel Malley as having been a garage mechanic, an insurance salesman, who wrote, but never published, the 'poems' found after his tragic death at the age of 25 by his sister, who sent them to *Angry Penguins* for an opinion of their worth.

We produced the whole of Ern Malley's tragic life-work in one afternoon, with the aid of a chance collection of books which happened to be on our desks: the *Concise Oxford Dictionary*, a *Collected Shakespeare, Dictionary of Quotations* &c.

We opened books at random, choosing a word or phrase haphazardly ... We deliberately perpetrated bad verse.

Some days after that October Saturday, Max Harris opened his mail and found a letter from an Ethel Malley of Croydon New South Wales that began:

Dear Sir,

When I was going through my brother's things after his death, I found some poetry he had written. I am no judge of it myself but a friend who I showed it to thinks it is very good and should be published. On his advice I am sending you some of the poems for an opinion.

Harris read the first poem, *Durer: Innsbruck, 1945*

I had often cowled in the slumberous heavy air,
Closed my inanimate lids to find it real,
As I knew it would be, the colourful spires
And painted roofs, the high snows glimpsed at the back,
All reversed in the quiet reflecting waters –
Not knowing then that Durer perceived it too.
Now I find that once more I have shrunk

> To an interloper, robber of dead men's dream,
> I had read in books that art is not easy
> But no one warned that the mind repeats
> In its ignorance the vision of others. I am still
> The black swan of trespass on alien waters.

Harris was awestruck. 'I was immediately impressed that here was a poet of tremendous power, working through a disciplined and restrained kind of statement into the deepest wells of human experience.'

At once he replied, asking for more poems and some biographical information. At the same time he wrote in some excitement to John Reed in Melbourne, his financial backer and the patron of Sidney Nolan, among others. 'Here's a pretty terrific discovery,' Harris wrote, 'I am certain that there is no gag in it ... it's too perfectly done ... among the most outstanding poems I have ever come across.' Reed and Nolan agreed.

And Ethel came back with 17 more poems, to be read in sequence under the title *The Darkening Ecliptic,* and a summary of Ern's sad life in a few hundred words. Briefly it described his poor performance at school, which he left early to become a garage mechanic; he had then gone to Melbourne where he sold insurance policies for National Mutual before coming back, fatally ill, to Sydney where Ethel nursed him until his death. He told her he had spent a lot of time in the Melbourne Public Library and she thought he had been fond of a girl in Melbourne but had some sort of differences with her. 'I am sorry I can't tell you much more about Ern.'

The sting, like all good confidence tricks, depended on Max Harris wanting to believe that the poetry he was sent was the work of a genius, the first great poetry to come from an Australian. He did without hesitation. And his enthusiasm was given impetus by the tantalising fact that Ern Malley had died of Graves' disease at 25. Ern's untimely end put him in the company of other poets of genius who had died young: Thomas Chatterton, a 19th-century literary hoaxer who poisoned himself at 17; John Keats, who died of tuberculosis at 26; and Percy Bysshe Shelley, who drowned at 30.

Harris was ecstatic. He wrote to Ethel offering payment for the poems. She refused. (McAuley and Stewart might have been liable to charges of taking money under false pretences.) He asked for more details of Ern's life and where he lived in Melbourne. And did she have photographs of Ern? Ethel replied saying that she thought Ern 'might have got into some sort of trouble in Melbourne and gone under another name'. She couldn't help with addresses other than the suburb of South Melbourne and neglected to respond to Harris's request for photographs. Nevertheless Harris decided to tell John Reed, who had urged him to ask for photographs, 'There are no photographs of Malley – the couple there were he deliberately destroyed on arriving in Sydney.'

There were sceptics who believed, in varying degrees, that the poems were a hoax. Harris, intoxicated with the standard of the poems and the tragedy of the poet, brushed them aside. In June 1944, he published the autumn issue of *Angry Penguins* with a colour cover illustration by Nolan, *The Sole Arabian Tree,* a line from one of the poems. And on 18 June, tipped off by a cadet journalist friend of Stewart's, the Sydney *Sunday Sun,* broke the story under the heading, 'Ern Malley, the great poet or the greatest hoax?'

The chuckles, the sniggers, the guffaws went round the English-speaking world. Here at last was someone holding up a mirror to the incomprehensible and absurd poetry of the moderns. The *Bulletin* of 5 July hailed 'the joint debunkers of Bosh and Blah and Blather', the Melbourne *Herald* editorialised, 'That much derided phrase, "I may not know much about art, but I know what I like," is good sense after all.'

Harris, mortified, hit back: 'Ern Malley was a fine poet but the two soldiers who created him are not.'

He was stretching a point but it was one that increasingly people began to lean to. McAuley and Stewart's creature overshadowed the hoax and now the literary world overseas began to take Malley's side.

Yes, the poems were knocked up in an afternoon, yes they were, sometimes, deliberately nonsensical, and yes they included lines from a report on the drainage of breeding grounds for mosquitoes. And yet Harris's original judgement, that they were written by 'a poet, moreover, with a cool, strong, sinuous feeling for language' couldn't be denied. Despite themselves, McAuley and Stewart had written strangely beautiful poems. The avant-garde monster they despised had turned on them and triumphed.

TE LAWRENCE and the Ambush of the Light Horse

I was in Halim's wet things, with a torn Hurani jacket, and was yet limping from the broken foot acquired when we blew up Jemal's train . . . Someone called out in Turkish. We walked on deafly, but a sergeant came after, and took me roughly by the arm, saying 'The Bey wants you' . . . They took away my belt, and my knife, made me wash myself carefully . . . Tomorrow, perhaps, leave would be permitted, if I fulfilled the Bey's pleasure this evening . . .

They took me upstairs to the Bey's room; or to his bedroom, rather. He was another bulky man, a Circassian himself, perhaps, and sat on the bed in a night-gown, trembling and sweating as though with fever. When I was pushed in he kept his head down, and waved the guard out. In a breathless voice he told me to sit on the floor in front of him, and after that was dumb; while I gazed at the top of his great head, on which the bristling hair stood up, no longer than the dark stubble on his cheeks and chin. At last he looked me over, and told me to stand up; and then to turn round. I obeyed; he flung himself back on the bed, and dragged me down with him in his arms. When I saw what he wanted I twisted around and up again, glad to find myself equal to him, at any rate in wrestling.

He began to fawn on me, saying how white and fresh I was, how fine my hands and feet, and how he would let me off drills and duties, make me his orderly, even pay me wages, if I would love him.

I was obdurate, so he changed his tone, and sharply ordered me to take off my drawers. When I hesitated, he snatched at me; and I pushed him back. He clapped his hands for the sentry, who hurried in and pinioned me. The Bey cursed me with horrible threats, and made the man holding me tear my clothes away, bit by bit.

And on and on for another 1000 words, TE Lawrence drools in this steamy bodice ripper that might be titled *In the Cruel Embrace of the Ottoman Bey*. It is a notorious episode in *The Seven Pillars of Wisdom*, Lawrence's account of his role in the World War I overthrow of the Turkish empire in the Middle East. Lawrence's masterpiece inspired the 1961 movie *Lawrence of Arabia* with Peter O'Toole playing Lawrence, all dilated blue eyes and quivering jaw muscles – no more so than when the greasy Bey was having his way – and Alec Guinness, this time under a dusky tan and the keffiyeh headdress of Feisal, the Arab prince.

Much of the book is tosh, as Lawrence later admitted to his biographer, Robert Frost. It just didn't happen. The nasty business with the Bey, for instance, is almost certainly a figment of a fervent imagination, Lawrence probably 100 kilometres away from where he claims it took place. That he was a homosexual there can be little doubt. He was also a masochist (he paid men to beat him), and he was very likely a sadist. In *Seven Pillars* he dwells far too long and with far too much relish on his execution of an Arab, describing the man's death down to the last agonised twitch. He also never denied urging Arabs to put to the sword unarmed Turkish prisoners.

He was illegitimate, something that mattered in his day and

particularly in the elite circle he moved in. And he was height-challenged – just 166 centimetres. But he had a towering ego and a writing style marked by hyperbole. 'I loved you, so I drew these tides of men into my hand and wrote my will across the sky in stars' Lawrence declared in his dedication of *Seven Pillars* to 'S.A.', presumably the 14-year-old Arab boy, Selim Ahmed, with whom he lived on an archaeological dig and took with him to England on holiday.

Purple prose and lust in the dunes is one thing. But Lawrence, who disliked Australians – 'ill-disciplined, low-life looters' – went too far when he grossly distorted historical events. *The Seven Pillars of Wisdom* concludes with his triumph; Lawrence and his Arab tribesmen liberating Damascus, the first troops into the fabled city that had fallen before him to such other great men as Ramses II, Alexander the Great and Napoleon.

In 1927, Lawrence admitted to Robert Graves, 'I was on thin ice when I wrote the Damascus chapter, SP *[Seven Pillars]* is full of half truths here,' – but by then Lawrence's rewriting of one of the landmark moments of World War I had been cemented. The lie has denied the Australian Light Horse their rightful place in history and has survived, indomitable and impregnable, for almost a century.

In truth, it was the Australians, under Lieutenant General Harry Chauvel, who first swept into Damascus, entering the city at 5 am on 1 October 1918, pushing through to pursue the Turks along the Aleppo road to their final surrender and clearing the way for the Arab army to enter Damascus later the same day. Lawrence arrived with them in the comfort of a Rolls-Royce, and the Commander-in-chief of the Egyptian Expeditionary Force, General Sir Edmund Allenby sent Chauvel a warm congratulatory telegram. Later, Allenby told Chauvel the race for Damascus was 'the greatest cavalry feat the world has ever known'.

But that's not the way Lawrence chose to remember it:

A galloping horseman checked at our head-cloths in the car, with a merry salutation, holding out a bunch of yellow grapes. 'Good news – Damascus salutes you.'

Nasir was just beyond us: to him we carried the tidings, that he might have the honourable entry, a privilege of his fifty battles. With Nuri Shaalan beside him, he asked a final gallop from his horse, and vanished down the long road in a cloud of dust, which hung reluctantly in the air between the water splashes. To give him a fair start, Stirling and I found a little stream, cool in the depths of a steep channel. By it we stopped, to wash and shave . . .

Quietly we drove up the long street to the Government buildings on the bank of the Barada. The way was packed with people, lined solid on the side-walks, in the road, at the windows and on the balconies or house-tops. Many were crying, a few cheered faintly, some bolder ones cried our names: but mostly they looked and looked, joy shining in their eyes. A movement like a long sigh from gate to heart of the city, marked our course . . .

They told me Chauvel was coming; our cars met in the southern outskirts. I described the excitement in the city, and how our new government could not guarantee administrative services before the following day, when I would wait on him, to discuss his needs and mine . . .

Chauvel . . . asked liberty for himself to drive round the town. I gave it so gladly that he asked if it would be convenient for him to make formal entry with his troops on the morrow. I said certainly . . .

Lieutenant General Chauvel, timidly asking Major Lawrence, five ranks below him, if he may be allowed to drive round the town? Harry Chauvel, who had commanded with such bravery at Gallipoli, the man who led 34,000 Anzac horsemen, who could ride and shoot with the best of them, who issued the order to charge at Beersheba, who won the Battle of Megiddo and followed it with an astonishing pursuit – 167 kilometres in three days to destroy the Turkish army and capture 31,335 prisoners – Chauvel asking Lawrence if it would be convenient for him to make formal entry with his troops the following day?

Chauvel wrote to his wife in Australia two days later:

We did not get within striking distance of Damascus until about 1 o'clock on the 30th. We were fighting all round the North, West and South of the city during the afternoon and night, Barrow having put in an appearance on the Southern Road, but did not get in (except for Grants Brigade [4th ALH Bde], temporarily under Bouchier, which got in to the Northern end of the city on the evening of the 30th) until about 6 o'clock on the morning of the 1st Oct. As soon as I knew my advance troops were in, I motored in to see the Wali to arrange about the civil administration . . .

The streets are strewn with dead men, camels and horses, and the main street was simply full of people who were very hard to get through in a car, despite the fact that we had a gun car in front of us. Rifle shots were going everywhere, mostly, I think in the air, and to add to the confusion, some of the wild Arabs from the Hedjaz, who had followed my advance troops in, were galloping about indiscriminately . . .

At the Government Offices I met Lawrence, the British political advisor to the King of the Hedjaz, who had also followed my advance troops in from the South. (I forbear to remark on this action of his as I might be trespassing against our censorship regulations.)

If only TE Lawrence had been so circumspect.

Awful ARTHUR ORTON, the Man Who Hoodwinked Two Nations

He was a grossly unattractive man. Obese, near illiterate, unabashedly belching and farting at will, afflicted with a twitch and with a tendency to drool, the butcher from Wagga Wagga was the type you find yourself next to on a very long plane flight in a very long nightmare.

She was the head of one of England's most illustrious families, one that had been prominent for a millennium, and the ninth richest in the land. The two had never met. Yet when Arthur Orton, the oafish butcher from Back o' Burke, arrived in Paris in 1867 to meet Lady Tichborne, the immensely wealthy dowager widow of the Baronet Sir Roger Tichborne, she 'recognised' him as her long lost son, Roger, and settled an annual allowance on him of £1000.

This was all very well. One thousand pounds a year was then a handy sum. At the time, labourers in Britain received around £30 a year. But it was just a fraction of the wealth that came with the family hereditary title. And Arthur Orton wanted to get his hands on that hereditary title.

The legal battle Orton instigated became one of the most

controversial and comical in British legal history. It had half the population of the British Isles and Australia 'the lower class' fervently convinced that this fat, uncouth man was indeed the aristocratic Roger Tichborne. And it had the other half outraged at the idea that a member of the aristocracy could so much as conceive of being a butcher in Wagga Wagga, Australia. His counsel put it down to 'uninterrupted sunshine in Australia . . . the kind of place that could seduce a man, make him forget his family and everything that was proper . . . a vagabond life, pleasant but wrong.'

All that was debatable. The real question was not whether Arthur Orton was Roger Tichborne, but how on earth did he manage to convince even one solitary soul that he was? In the annals of confidence trickery, there is nothing to touch the monumental audacity of the butcher from Wagga Wagga.

The trial to determine the truth about the Tichborne Claimant was one of the first 'celebrity trials', and until the 1997 McLibel case fought by McDonalds, the longest running legal action in British history. The cost was colossal. Around the world it was followed with intense interest. An army of witnesses for both sides was cross-examined by the finest jurists of the time. Outside the court on some days, more than 10,000 people milled. Yet the whole matter could have been resolved in an instant. Roger Tichborne had tattoos on both arms. Arthur Orton had none. Yet nobody inexplicably thought to ask the Tichborne Claimant to bare his arms.

Roger Tichborne was born in Paris in 1829, the eldest son of an English baronet. Arthur Orton was born in 1834, the son of an English butcher. Apart from that, they had nothing in common. Roger was educated in Paris and grew up speaking French as his first language. Arthur was educated in inner London's Wapping, and grew up speaking Cockney as his first language.

At 15, Roger was sent to England to study at the famous Jesuit school, Stonyhurst. At 19, he obtained his commission in the renowned 6th Dragoon Guards, the Carabineers, and fell in love with his cousin, Catherine Doughty, and she with him. At around the same time, young Arthur Orton was apprenticed at sea in the hope of curing him of the curious nervous condition, St Vitus's Dance. His family thought that a return sea voyage to South America might cause it to disappear. Instead, Arthur disappeared. At Valparaiso, in Chile, he jumped ship – life at sea for a boy was brutal – and lived anonymously and out of touch with his family in the little town of Melipilla where a family called Castro befriended the young gringo. Then, after 18 months, he sailed home.

Meanwhile, Roger had resigned his commission his men made fun of him and fallen out with his family over Catherine. His parents, who were at odds with each other, were united in their opposition to the marriage, and in 1853, Roger left for South America in something of a huff. In June, he arrived in Valparaiso, Arthur's old stamping ground. A month earlier, Arthur Orton had stepped off a ship at Hobart Town in Van Diemen's Land. Arthur, too, had gone to sea again after his parents opposed his wishes to marry a girl named Mary Ann Loder.

From Chile, Roger travelled to Peru, Buenos Aires and Rio de Janeiro, all the while sending his mother and other relatives letters and travel souvenirs – stuffed birds, animal skins and the like. In 1854, a year after he had said goodbye to the family seat in Hampshire, Roger sailed in the *Bella*, bound for Kingston, Jamaica. He never arrived. The *Bella* was lost at sea with all hands; only an upturned longboat and debris were ever found.

Lady Tichborne, however, would not accept that her firstborn child was gone. (Around this time, Charles Dickens created the character of Miss Havisham, the spurned bride who could never accept that she had been left waiting at the church. Miss Havisham would have applauded Lady Tichborne's stubborn refusal to face the facts.) She resolutely forbade any talk that her boy was dead and kept a lamp light burning metaphorically and literally for his return.

To this light, burning through the night in the entrance at Tichborne Park, came vagabond sailors, rogues and down-on-their-luck wanderers who had heard that Lady Tichborne wanted to believe that her son was alive. They would regale her with stories of shipwrecked survivors and leave with a shilling or two in their pocket. Her husband, Sir James Tichborne, was intensely irritated by her blind optimism, but this may have only strengthened her resolve. Lady Tichborne and Sir James were constantly fighting and she loathed his family. When he died in 1862, and when Roger's only brother, Alfred, followed four years later, she stepped things up. She began to advertise for news of Roger. The personal section of classified advertisements columns in newspaper around the world carried insertions such as this:

> A HANDSOME REWARD will be given to any person who can furnish such information as will discover the fate of ROGER CHARLES TICHBOURNE. He sailed from the port of Rio Janeiro on the 20th of April, 1854, in the ship La Bella, and has never been heard of since, but a report reached England to the effect that a portion of the crew and passengers of vessel of that name was picked up by a vessel bound to Australia Melbourne it is believed it is not known whether the said ROGER CHARLES TICHBORNE was amongst the drowned or saved. He would at the present time be about 32 years of age; is of a delicate constitution, rather tall, with very light brown hair and blue eyes.

The description of Roger Tichborne was not wholly accurate. He would have been 36, not 32, he wasn't tall, and his hair was black, not very light brown. (Arthur Orton's hair was brown with a reddish hue.) But the hint of a fragile soul is echoed in a daguerreotype photograph taken around the time he set sail from England. It shows a twerp. A limp, wistful gentleman who gives every appearance of being, perhaps, an enthusiastic collector of railway timetables.

Arthur Orton, on the other hand, tipped the scale at way over 124 kilograms, and at his peak weighed in at an enormous 171 kilograms. Where Roger Tichborne had, it was said, 'walked like a Frenchman', Arthur Orton was stooped and shambling. And where Roger had been mocked by his men in the Carabineers, Arthur was a gent who had been around. After his arrival in Hobart Town, Arthur spent the next 13 years living, sometimes on the wrong side of the law, in various places around Australia. In 1859, he was digging for gold at Reedy Creek, New South Wales, when he heard there was a warrant for his arrest for horse stealing. Orton disappeared once more and reappeared in Wagga Wagga, NSW, working as a butcher and calling himself Tom Castro the surname of the family who looked after him in Melipilla, Chile. As Tom Castro, he married Mary Ann Bryant in 1865.

Wagga Wagga was a town of around 1000 inhabitants, one of them a solicitor named Gibbes. Among his clients was Orton, who had gone bankrupt, but who was in the habit of telling people that he was from a famous titled family back in England and that his name was not really Castro. Gibbes used to drink with Orton, and his interest in Orton's alleged links with English aristocracy was fired when Orton asked if property in England to which he was entitled would have to be included in the bankruptcy. It was fuelled further when Orton casually dropped a titbit of intriguing information he had been shipwrecked at sea, he claimed.

When the solicitor got home and told Mrs Gibbes what Orton had told him, her feminine intuition put two and two together: Tom Castro must be the missing heir she had read about in advertisements in the *Sydney Morning Herald*. When the question was put to him, Orton would not confirm or deny that he was the man. That was enough for Gibbes to write to Arthur Cubbit, the proprietor of the Missing Friends Agency, who had placed the advertisement. The Tichborne Claimant juggernaut was under way.

Arthur Orton, at the suggestion of Gibbes, wrote a letter to Lady Tichborne in which he claimed he had arrived in Melbourne on 24 July 1854, after being rescued from the *Bella* by a ship named *Osprey* and had since lived under the name of Castro. He apologised for 'the trubl and anxsity [sic]' his long absence had caused. (The real Roger, like Orton, had also been no great shakes with the English language.)

Orton intended, he confessed years later, simply to get enough money to see him and his wife and child out of the country. 'The reason I wrote the letter was because I was hard pressed for money at the time, and I thought that if she was fool enough to send me money so much the better. I could go to Sydney and take the steamer to Panama where I could join my brother and nobody would ever hear anything from me.'

But Lady Tichborne declined to send money. She wrote to Mr Cubitt: 'You do not give any details whatever about the person you believe to be my son, you do not name even the town where he is, and you do not say anything about the way he was saved from the shipwreck.' Her interest, however, was roused. One of the stories she had been told about the loss of the *Bella* was that it had not been sunk at all, but stolen by a mutinous crew who renamed it, repainted it and sailed it to Australia. Lady Tichborne offered 200 pounds to cover the voyage to England if Cubbit and Gibbes could provide some proof. She herself accelerated matters by recommending that Gibbes and Cubitt get in touch with an old former servant of the Tichbornes, Andrew Bogle, a West Indian who had been rescued from slavery by Roger's uncle. Bogle had been given an annuity by the family and retired to Sydney. Tichborne Park's former head gardener, Michael Guilfoyle, was also in Sydney. Both had known Roger now the baronet, Sir Roger, if indeed he were alive.

At this stage, the game should have been up for the Wagga Wagga butcher. Instead he and his harridan wife and child went to Sydney – he had little to lose after all – and found to his amazement and intense delight that they were treated like royalty. Then Bogle arrived. It took him only a few minutes to pronounce that the large fat man before him was indeed the slim young man he had known. After all, Bogle reasoned, Sir Roger had at once recognised him and he had such knowledge of Sir Roger's family and background that he must be the missing baronet. Guilfoyle the gardener came to the same conclusion. And both of them wrote to Lady Tichborne telling her so.

Andrew Bogle was no fool. He could not possibly have believed that the man Castro was Roger Tichborne. Almost certainly he did a deal with Castro. He would teach Castro the social skills a gentleman such as Roger would have, and he would brief him on all possible details of the Tichborne family and the events surrounding Roger's disappearance. In return he would be employed, once more as a valet, at Tichborne Park, a life far more luxurious than that he knew in Sydney.

Arthur Orton, too, was no fool. Near illiterate, yes, coarse and uncouth, yes, but he was intelligent and quick. He had a real talent for rhetoric and a vivid imagination, possibly aided by the nervous condition, St Vitus's Dance, which left its physical legacy in his twitch. And he had just enough knowledge, from letters Lady Tichborne had sent, from *Burke's Peerage* and from newspaper articles, to start a conversation and then get the other person talking. He retained what he was told and repeated it to the next person, in turn gathering more information.

Years later, in a confession he wrote for publication in *The People*, Orton claimed that Andrew Bogle was genuine in his belief. Awful though he appeared on the surface, Arthur Orton was a decent bloke deep down.

Bogle thoroughly believed I was Sir Roger, he used to converse very freely with me about the family, giving me the whole history of it . . . I was pumping him all the time as to names and habits and customs of various members of the family. I have always been a good listener and by listening quietly and patiently for hours, to statements which have been made to me by, I suppose, many hundreds of people, all of whom gave information concerning the Tichborne family, I learned such facts that really induced me to prosecute my claim. I found by listening to others the story built itself and grew so large I really couldn't get out of it.

With the assurance of Bogle, the faithful old servant, Lady Tichborne now threw aside all caution and wrote to Castro urging him to hurry to England. To Gibbes, she confided: 'I think my poor, dear Roger confuses everything in his mind, and I believe him to be my son, though his statements differ from mine.'

On Christmas Day 1866, the Tichborne Claimant arrived in England. Almost his first action had been to visit the Globe Inn, Wapping, where he made inquiries 'on behalf of an old friend Arthur Orton back in Australia'. His father, George, had been a butcher on High Street, Wapping, and had 12 children, and Arthur needed to buy their silence.

Next Orton and his party travelled to Paris where his 'mother' Lady Tichbourne had summoned him. In a darkened room in the Place de la Madeleine, he lay fully dressed on a bed, too unwell to see his 'mamma'. She came anyway. She bent down and kissed him. 'He looks like his father and his ears are like his uncle's,' she said, like a proud mother looking at her newborn child for the first time. The claimant was sick with worry that he was about to be denounced. Instead Lady Tichborne declared, in the presence of a doctor, that the man in the bed was her firstborn son.

The dowager was delighted. The servants hadn't seen her laugh in years. She and Castro were inseparable, and for weeks they walked and talked. Arthur Orton, when making a will before setting out for England, had got Lady Tichborne's name completely wrong, but the dowager was unfussed by any mistakes he made or questions he was at a loss to answer. He could remember nothing of his childhood: the names of his friends, his favourite dogs, books he had read even the fact that he couldn't speak French, his native tongue, didn't faze her. A head injury in the shipwreck, illness, alcoholism and the passage of time, all accounted for these lapses, she insisted.

Then Lady Tichborne died. The Tichborne estates now belonged to the infant son of Roger's brother, Arthur. This left Orton in a pickle. Either he had to drop the pretence and seek anonymity perhaps, as he was later to reveal, in Panama or he had to fight to establish that he was Roger, the heir to the Tichborne estates. Naturally, he chose to go for broke. In his published confession, Arthur Orton gives a plausible glimpse into this thought process.

> I could not get away from those who were infatuated with me and firmly believed I was the Real Sir Roger . . . Of course I knew perfectly well I was not, but they made so much of me, and persisted in addressing me as Sir Roger, that I forgot who I was and by degree I began to believe I was really the rightful owner of the estates. If it had not been that I was feted and made so much of by the colonists of Sydney I should have taken the boat and gone the rest of my days to Panama with my brother.

The trial of the century that followed Arthur Orton's decision to legally establish he was Sir Roger involved the most eminent jurists of the day in what was, until the 1990s, the longest running legal action in British history. It remains the most expensive. It was watched with fascination around the world. Gilbert and Sullivan based *Trial by Jury* on the case. Mark Twain was so inspired by Orton that he used him as a model for some characters in *Huckleberry Finn*. It was the best show in town – far funnier and with more twists and dramatic developments than anything on in the West End. Before each session, the streets outside the court were crowded with people trying to get a seat in the public galleries. European royalty took their turn in the ticket queue.

The court case was, at times, pure *Monty Python*. Here is the exchange between the Solicitor General, Sir John Coleridge, and Orton regarding his claim to have studied Latin, Greek and Hebrew (a course not on the curriculum at Stonyhurst).

> Coleridge: 'Can you read Hebrew now?'
> Orton (triumphantly): 'Not a word!'
> 'Have you studied Greek?'
> 'Yes.'
> 'Did your studies in Greek go as far as the alphabet?'
> 'I don't know.'
> 'You surely remember that?'
> 'I went there unprepared.'
> 'Could you make out Greek at that time?'
> 'Perhaps a sentence.'
> 'Could you read the first chapter of St John?'
> 'No.'
> 'Does any of it linger in your mind now?'
> 'Not a bit of it.'
> 'Could you give us the Greek for "and"?'
> 'No, and I'm not going to do anything of the kind.'
> 'Did you get on better with Latin?'
> 'I believe I got further in Latin.'
> 'Was Caesar a Latin writer or a Greek writer?'
> 'I can't say. I suppose it was Greek.'

Laughter in court. There was often laughter in court and often it was led by the Claimant. No-one laughed more loudly or seemed less agitated about the outcome than the man in the dock this 'great body of evidence' as one counsel sneered. (Orton had by this time blown to elephantine girth.)

The game seemed up. But then the claimant's solicitors played their ace: a sailor from the *Osprey* named Jean Luie. He told the court that he had helped rescue the claimant from the sinking ship and nursed him back to health. The claimant, he said, had told him his name was Sir Roger Tichborne.

Jean Luie, the Good Samaritan of the sea, was, however, better known to the police as a confidence trickster named Sorensen, and, exposed after two days cross-examination, made a run for it. Sorensen was jailed for perjury – seven years in his case. Jailed too, were others who were found to have perjured themselves for the claimant.

Arthur Orton's brother Charles, like his two sisters, at first denied that the claimant was known to him. (Orton was bribing all three.) But in court he identified the claimant as his brother.

A Dr Lipscombe, described as Sir Roger's personal physician, gave evidence of a rare physical defect that, he said, distinguished Sir Roger. The young aristocrat, he said, had an abnormal penis. It regressed, like a horse's, into his body. The claimant, Thomas Castro, had that same abnormality.

Was there to be no end to the sensations in court? Suddenly there was. Under cross-examination Dr Lipscombe admitted that he had seen Sir Roger only twice, and that he had failed to disclose his association with friends of the claimant. And when Arthur Orton's sweetheart of years ago, Mary Anne Loder was called, she drove another nail into the case that was now a coffin.

Not only did Mary Anne identify the man in the dock as her old flame Arthur, the Wapping butcher boy, she also gave evidence that in the course of the courtship she had become acquainted with Arthur Orton's penis – at times it regressed into his body, she recalled. A pocketbook belonging to Tom Castro was tendered in evidence. Among the addresses in the book was Mary Anne Loder's.

It had always been inevitable that the Tichborne Claimant would lose the case, and it followed inevitably that he was charged with perjury. Orton's trial began in 1873, and 10 months later, he was sentenced to 14 years' penal servitude. He was released from prison in 1884, a changed man. He wrote and had published his confession, but to the delight of students of the case and many authors who were later to make money from the confidence trick of the century, he later retracted it. Naturally, he took to the boards; as 'The Tichborne Claimant' he performed a wretched parody of himself for music hall audiences who delighted in pelting him with rotten fruit. The same people throwing tomatoes had wanted to rescue him from jail and carry him to freedom when he was convicted. And, to this day, there are those who still believe Arthur Orton was the missing baronet. There was something about Arthur that attracted admiration and belief.

Orton died on April Fools' Day 1898. At the end, Arthur Orton had finally come clean. He had revealed himself as a likeable man.

THE STINGS

A confidence game planned and executed with care

THE SPORT OF KINGS – and Knaves

The colourful Sydney racing identity, as the criminal George Freeman was euphemistically called, sometimes arranged, it was said, for every horse but one to run 'dead' in a race. Is this possible? Can *every* jockey be bribed to ride to a plan that will lead to only one, preordained, winner? And to do this in a way that it will not arouse undue suspicion?

It can be done. As we saw at Flemington in 1983.

'And they're off in the 1930 Melbourne Cup!' the course broadcaster bellowed in that reedy Australian accent of 80 years ago, and those of us at Flemington that day in 1983 felt the thrill that only the Cup Day brings and began cheering for Phar Lap.

We were 'extras' dressed in the manner of the 1930s and urging on the horse playing Phar Lap in the movie of the same name. The movie's star, Towering Inferno, like Phar Lap, was a giant chestnut thoroughbred gelding. Towering Inferno had movie-star looks, but he was 10 years old, six years older than Phar Lap had been in 1930. And he was slow. The question was, could the jockeys arrange it so that Towering Inferno would streak clear in the straight and win by five lengths, as Phar Lap had?

No worries. The race was precisely choreographed. The *So You Think You Can Dance* judges would have been ecstatic. But to the onlookers at Flemington that day it appeared to be a genuine contest, with every horse and every jockey striving to get to the post first.

When Simon Wincer, *Phar Lap*'s director, called, 'That's a wrap!' and we drifted from the course, we'd learned a lesson. A lesson that some would take to heart and never again go near a racecourse.

They were fixing races in Australia in Phar Lap's time and long before. The first Melbourne Cup, in 1861, had the *Sydney Morning Herald* trembling with righteousness: 'It is the worst occasion and cause for a national gathering, that is naturally allied to more that makes directly for human degradation than any other public sport or pastime that could be named. The spirit of gambling hangs upon its skirts and penetrates to its heart.'

The *Herald* was getting into a terrible syntactic tangle and muddling its metaphors over the hardy perennial – the mutual loathing of Sydney and Melbourne, old even then in 1861 – and using a sports event, the Melbourne Cup, to disturb the skirts of the wicked younger sister to the south.

To which the younger sister city responded, *yah boo sucks!* Or words to that effect: 'Let us think for a moment. Is there any racing in New South Wales? Yes, there is; something on a level with our "Wallaby Flat" or Narrican Valley meetings . . . Poor Sydney.'

The Melbourne Cup has been front-page news for a century and half. But in the same time span, scandals and race fixes have been providing newspapers with many more front-page stories.

Forty-two years after a stallion named Archer won the first Cup, a horse called Gentleman Jim, named, possibly, in honour of the recent world heavyweight champion but more likely ironically in honour of his owner, Jim Kingsley, kept winning races under ever-increasing weights. The bookies were baffled. They kept betting against him. He – surely – couldn't keep on winning under those weights. But Gentleman Jim kept on saluting the judges. In April at Newcastle he won again with 68 kilograms on his back. On the way to the scales for his horse's weight to be declared, Kingsley, known as the Grafter, was accosted by an irate bookmaker. When he arrived late at the weigh-in the stewards told him that Gentleman Jim had weighed in 13 kilograms light.

The Grafter was outraged. Stomping around the scales he demanded that the jockey and his saddle be weighed again in front of him. This time the scales showed the correct weight. The bewildered clerk of the scales wondered: would the scales show the same correct weight if they were moved to another, perhaps more even surface? The scales were moved, revealing a small hole bored into the floorboard. Through it was a wire attached to the scales, and at the other end of the wire hung a lead weight. Also attached to the wire, under the floor, was a small boy. He was eating a pie when he was disturbed by the clerk of the scales. The small boy, who had responded to the Grafter's stomping cue, was responsible for Gentleman Jim's 'correct weight'.

Even more audacious was Harry Solomons's celebrated Phantom Call.

In 1939, at Melbourne's Ascot Racecourse, the landlines of four radio stations broadcasting the last race were cut just as the horses were about to jump. Only Harry Solomons on 3XY had a live line. Solomons went through the field as if the horses were still at the barrier. He kept focusing on the 6 to 1 shot, Buoyancy, ridden by Scobie Breasley. Buoyancy was playing up. Buoyancy wouldn't go to the barrier. Scobie was having trouble with Buoyancy, it was all about Buoyancy.

By now, of course, in real time, Buoyancy had won the race and those few punters in the know around Australia had got the message and plunged heavily. Then Solomons rapped, 'They're off!' and proceeded to broadcast a phantom call of the race he had previously seen, giving all the placings in the correct order.

He might have got away with it. But then it struck: hadn't 3DB's Eric Welch just called, 'They're racing' when his line was cut? And hadn't Solomons gone on talking for a minute or so after that before *he* called, 'They're off!'? Harry Solomons, who was deeply in debt to bookies, scooted immediately after his call. He was found six months later in Suva. He got six months' jail.

Harry got off lightly. Mel Schumacher, 'the Shoe', got a lifetime. A great and nerveless jockey, the Shoe was riding desperately on a horse called Blue Era in the 1961 AJC Derby at Randwick, getting his mount first to the post in a furious neck-and-neck scramble up the straight. No-one saw anything unusual.

As the jockeys pulled up their horses, Tommy Hill, on the second placegetter, yelled to George Moore, 'Schuie grabbed me by the leg! I'm going to protest, I'm going to!'

Moore yelled back, as though the whole idea of one jockey grabbing another's leg was absurd, 'Oh you're mad! Where did he pull your leg?'

'In the straight.'

The chief steward Jack Burke questioned Hill, who said, 'Oh, he grabbed my leg Mr Burke.'

'Are you sure Hill?'

'Mr Burke, I'd know if a snake bit me.'

The chief steward turned to 'the Shoe'. 'What have you got to say Schumacher?'

And Schumacher said, 'Well that's preposterous.'

He had a point. The two horses were locked together, thundering down the straight at 60 kilometres an hour and for one man to reach down and pull another's leg in front of 80,000 spectators – and get away with it – would seem ridiculous.

But that day, for the first time in Australia, technicians had installed 'patrol footage' technology. The cameraman had only just managed to get the camera working as they turned for home and Schumacher, along with the other jockeys, had no idea he was being recorded. The stewards ran the film.

'I couldn't believe it. I couldn't believe they had one,' the Shoe said years later. 'It was just one of those things. You see bike riders do it, you see runners do it and it just, this time it just happened to be on film and we got caught. What can't speak can't lie. I walked off the track with a life ban before the last. There was 80,000 people there and you could have heard a pin drop. It was like a funeral . . . my funeral.'

His life ban was later reduced to just six years.

Fourteen years on in the 'Kalgoorlie sting' the flamboyant Perth merchant banker entrepreneur, Laurie Connell, backed a Victorian horse in the interstate ring at Kalgoorlie, knowing, because of a delayed broadcast, the winner of the race.

In 1983, he was linked to the farce at Bunbury when jockey Danny Hobby slid off the favourite, Strike Softly, just after the gates opened. Danny wanted to make absolutely sure his horse lost. Hobby said he was paid $5000 by Connell to hop off the horse and then paid another $1 million have a long overseas holiday: several years long.

'He was the best travel agent I'd ever dealt with,' Danny reminisced fondly. 'I mean I used to ring from somewhere, I'd be sitting in London, laying in bed still and I'd decide . . . I might go to France or Switzerland. So I'd pack my case and make a phone call and by the time I got to the airport there'd be a ticket there waiting for me. I mean . . . you couldn't ask for better.'

Alas for Danny, his next accommodation, on his return to Australia, was a jail cell. In 1988, Strike Softly's trainer confessed to the fix. Connell was sentenced to five years' imprisonment for perverting the course of justice by paying Hobby to stay out of the country. Hobby got three years.

Connell served one year in jail before receiving a work release. But the year before the Strike Softly truth emerged Connell was involved in a scam that sickened the nation.

In the 1987 Perth Cup, Connell's horse Rocket Racer lived up to its name in spectacular fashion, winning by nine lengths and doing almost another lap of the course before it could be pulled up. Connell had backed the horse months out at long odds – from as much as 50-1 he claimed, and saw it start as the 2-1 favourite. He won $1.2 million.

Rocket Racer was clearly supercharged – injected with etorphine 'elephant juice' was the common verdict – and collapsed after the race. Racegoers Australia-wide watched aghast as several track attendants struggled to keep the horse on his feet. No swab was carried out as it was considered to be too dangerous to the horse, and Rocket Racer died from unknown causes a month later.

Rocket Racer was a scam carried out in full view. It was scandalous and sickening. But it paled compared to the Fine Cotton ring-in, a scam that ensured that horse's name would be forever remembered.

FINE COTTON and the Sting in the Horse's Tale

Oh, the Owner told Clarence the clocker
The clocker told jockey McGee
The jockey, of course, passed it on to the horse
And the horse told me
– From the film *Riding High* (1950) Johnny Burke/James Van Hensen

Horses can't talk of course, but dogs can bark and on 18 August 1984, the dogs were barking, 'Get on Fine Cotton!'

The comically inept scam that became known around the world as the Fine Cotton Affair might have starred Manuel and Basil from *Faulty Towers*, or Laurel and Hardy – 'Well, that's another fine mess you've gotten me into!' – but it had deeper and darker ramifications than the simple substitution of horses to bring home a colossal plunge. Reputations were ruined and there was a whiff of the underworld with one brutal murder and alleged threats of another.

Many have long suspected that there was a deeper 'double scam' in the Fine Cotton ring-in. A sting in the tail of the scam. It was said that George Freeman, the notorious Sydney SP bookie had known of the ring-in and, sure that it would be discovered and Fine Cotton disqualified, had backed Harbour Gold, the horse that finished second and was subsequently awarded the race.

In May 2010, the *Sunday Herald Sun* published Adam Shand's interview with John 'the Phantom' Gillespie, the man at the centre of the ring-in. Gillespie claimed that he and his syndicate had backed Harbour Gold, knowing that the ring-in would be rumbled – by his own men if necessary. Gillespie said he had been put up to it by a Sydney SP bookie and drug dealer, 'Melbourne Mick' Sayers, who was later murdered by a rival dealer.

Whatever the truth, one thing is certain. The farcical ring-in of 1984 had not the slightest chance of succeeding. Gillespie and Hayden Haitana, Fine Cotton's trainer, wittingly or unwittingly, made sure of that.

Gillespie is a man who, as they say in turf circles and law enforcement agencies, has 'form'. At last count, in 2008, when he was in the news again for shady dealings, he had around 350 convictions for various offences including false pretences, stealing, and the armed hold-up of a Brisbane TAB. Gillespie got three years for that back in the early eighties. In Brisbane's Boggo Road Goal in 1983, he hatched a sting – a ring-in, substituting a good horse for a proven no-hoper and backing it to win.

It was not a novel idea; ring-ins are part of the lure and lore of the turf. How many ring-ins have succeeded is impossible to calculate – we'll never know – but those that fail pop up once or twice a decade and are then largely forgotten. Gillespie himself had tried it two years earlier, in 1982, at Doomben Racecourse. The horse, racing under the false name of Mannasong, opened at 66-1 and started at 9-2. 'Mannasong' ran like a 66-1 shot and finished eighth. The trainer was barred for life. Gillespie told his cell mate, the jockey Pat Haitana, that he was looking for a trainer who could organise a ring-in that couldn't fail. Haitana recommended his brother, Hayden, who trained a plodder called Fine Cotton in Coffs Harbour, New South Wales.

Hayden Haitana was a battler with a small string of horses. He liked a drink, and, it transpired when he was subsequently apprehended, had a fondness for white suits of the kind then favoured by Queensland Members of Parliament and Kentucky Fried Chickens' Colonel Sanders. Fine Cotton, too, was a battler, a nine-year-old bay gelding, a horse that was almost invariably listed as 'also ran' in around 70 race results, most of them picnic races. And Dashing Solitaire, the third party to the swindle, was a six-year-old bay gelding who looked very much like Fine Cotton. But he was a Group Two winner and, in that sense, a horse of a very different colour. Gillespie had paid $10,000 for the horse, he said, with money given to him by Mick Sayers, the Sydney drug dealer and SP bookie.

Dashing Solitaire was set to take Fine Cotton's place and the fix was on until a kangaroo entered the picture. It bounded across Dashing Solitaire's path, causing the bay to rear and stumble into a barbed wire fence. Badly injured, Dashing Solitaire had to be scratched from the scam.

Up until now things had gone smoothly. The sensible thing to do would have been to postpone the ring-in until they could find another body double for Fine Cotton. But Gillespie couldn't wait and bought another bay gelding, Bold Personality.

The bay looked nothing like Fine Cotton. Bold Personality had a 4/7 brand on his shoulder, while Fine Cotton had a 1/6 brand. Bold Personality was much lighter in colour and had a white star on his head. Fine Cotton didn't. Fine Cotton had white socks on his rear legs. Bold Personality didn't. Bold Personality was a Group Two winner. Fine Cotton was heading for the pet food factory.

There were three days to go before the big race and Tomaso di Luzio went to Coffs Harbour to bring Bold Personality to Brisbane. Di Luzio threw a heavy winter blanket over Bold Personality for the six-hour ride in the heat and humidity.

By the time di Luzio got to Brisbane, Bold Personality was dehydrating. Haitana decided the horse needed to be drenched, a procedure usually performed only by a vet involving water flushed into the horse's stomach through a hose inserted into a nostril. Bold Personality, not surprisingly, began to bleed heavily from his nose. Haitana had the answer to this: he had the horse's head lashed upright to the rafters of the stables.

It was time to call in the make-up artists. Gillespie and Haitana went to a pharmacy and set to work with Clairol hair dye peroxide and enamel paint.

The following morning, the day of the race, Haitana inspected his work. Bold Personality was now not a dark bay brown but red. Bright, flaming red. They set off for the track with both horses, stopping at a home where Bold Personality was hosed down in the front garden in an attempt to wash out the red. They arrived at Eagle Farm an hour before the race. Fine Cotton was left out in his float in the car park; he was needed on the spot to be switched in case there were slip ups – hard to imagine, but the best-laid plans can go wrong. And Haitana covered Bold Personality with a blanket, to try to hide his colour for as long as possible.

Fine Cotton's jockey was not in on the sting and was puzzled to see other jockeys in the mounting yard winking at him. More puzzling, the trainer had wanted the horse blanketed until it got to the barriers.

Now, the Commerce Novice (2nd division) Handicap over 1500 metres was about to get under way. Bold Personality, doped on uppers to the tip of his tail, red paint dripping under his blanket, made his way to the barrier. In the bar, Hayden Haitana was drinking heavily and around the nation betting rings were in a frenzy. The ring-in whisper had become a deafening roar. The bookies and the TAB had opened with Fine Cotton at 33-1 but at the starting stalls Fine Cotton had come in at 6-4. Harbour Gold, the favourite before the dogs barked the news of the ring-in, had drifted out to 5-1.

And they're racing! [Eagle Farm race caller:] Fine Cotton's still the leader, he's about a neck in front. Harbour Gold's coming at him solidly now. Fine Cotton and Harbour Gold, they're going to fight it out. Harbour Gold's just about got his nose in front, Fine Cotton's kicking again on the inside. Fine Cotton and Harbour Gold. Fine Cotton's in front. They're drawing to the line. He's just in front – Fine Cotton and Harbour Gold lunge right on the line! They hit it! Pretty tight this one. Fine Cotton or Harbour Gold – it could go either way, then Cabaret Kingdom.

They were screaming 'Ring-in! Ring-in!' before Bold Personality/Fine Cotton came back to the scale, paint running down his fetlocks. The stewards' warning siren blared: no payout on the winning horse. One theory has it that the men bellowing 'ring-in!' were George Freeman's stooges. John Gillespie told Adam Shand in 2010 that it was his men. Either way the jig was up.

'Fine Cotton' was stripped of the race a half-hour later as the stewards searched fruitlessly for Haitana and Gillespie. Haitana was found two weeks later in South Australia. He told his story to *60 Minutes*. In his interview he said he had been a reluctant participant in the fraud and claimed that an anonymous telephone caller had threatened that if he didn't go along he would 'end up like George Brown'. George Brown was also a trainer, who had been horrifically tortured, murdered and set alight in his car near Wollongong on 2 April 1984. His killing was almost certainly in retaliation for his failure to proceed with a ring-in swindle.

Haitana was warned-off for life and jailed for 12 months. Gillespie, like Haitana, ran for cover immediately after the race and was not found until November the next year when police opened a cupboard door in his sister's house in Cobham, Victoria. He was sentenced to four years' jail.

The racing industry in Queensland and NSW, particularly,

was rocked by the Fine Cotton Affair. But when it emerged that the bookmakers Bill Waterhouse and his son Robbie were implicated, the tremors went around the nation. The Waterhouses were racing royalty but they were found to have had prior knowledge of the ring-in and were given life bans – warned-off racecourses worldwide. The bans were lifted in 1998 when Robbie Waterhouse admitted to the Thoroughbred Racing Board that he had a week's prior knowledge of the ring-in, and that his conduct had been dishonourable, dishonest and disgraceful

Yet the decision bewildered Bill. 'To this day, I still wonder how anyone in their right mind could ever think that Rob and I would have been mixed up with such fools,' Waterhouse said in his autobiography, *What Are the Odds?*

In his book, Bill Waterhouse explained how some of the bets were laid:

> I later learnt that Gary Clarke, who was working for Rob as a clerk, had asked Rob to put a commission on [Fine Cotton] for an unknown party and Rob had added a bit of his own. Rob arranged to send a clerk up to Gosford to put some money on, and on the spur of the moment gave some money and a tip to poor Father O'Dwyer, who, looking to make some money for his holidays, backed it himself. I am sure no-one would pass on a tip like that if they thought there was something hot afoot.

'Poor Father O'Dwyer', a keen punter removed from his parish when he introduced gambling nights, had been in the news four years before. At the 1980 NSW Royal Commissions into drug trafficking, Justice Woodward found that the Wings Travel company, of which Father Edward Brian O'Dwyer was founding director, had been involved in drug trafficking – its clients were 'a manifest who's who of drug traffickers' – but he could not conclude that Father O'Dwyer and fellow principal Paul Dole were involved. Justice

Woodward was keen to interview Dole, but he had disappeared.

The Waterhouses and others appealed against the warnings off. Judge Alf Goran at the Racing Appeals Tribunal, whom Bill had thought a friend (they'd gone to law school together), was scathing:

> The bettors, Murray, Clarke, Mrs Clarke, McCoy, Hines, Gough and O'Dwyer were each said to have acted in a way, both in backing a horse like Fine Cotton in the first place and by doing so in a very strange fashion. Those would demonstrate a link between them . . . Secondly, all of these persons were associates of RW Waterhouse, either as friends, in business, employment or habit on the racecourse . . . The committee in fact came to believe because of his position in racing and his influence with these persons he was the controller of the [betting] operation.

Of Father O'Dwyer's story, Goran said, 'The whole story is contrived.' Of Gary Clarke's explanation of why he backed Fine Cotton, Goran said it was 'sheer nonsense . . . Mr Clarke's story is completely ruined by the fact his wife made a special journey the same morning to Southport to back Fine Cotton. The whole of this is a fairy story to be told around a roaring fire on a later afternoon during winter.'

Horses can't talk. But can horses laugh? They may say neigh, and it's a moot point, but if they can, Fine Cotton had the last laugh. When he died on a Toowoomba property in February 2009, he was 31, a venerable age. And for most of his long life he had enjoyed as much fame as any of the thoroughbred greats of his time. His name will live on long after most of them are forgotten. And all for winning a race without leaving the horse float.

THE DECEPTIONS

A ruse; a trick

How HORRIE the Wog Dog Fooled Us All

Horrie the Wog Dog's execution shocked a nation and became part of our folklore. A brave little dog, a hero to thousands of servicemen who had fought alongside him, 'destroyed' by the hands of a vicious and petty bureaucracy. That is what we have believed for six decades and that is why for many years wreaths were laid in his honour on Anzac Day.

But did Horrie really die? Or did he hoodwink the nation and live, in an identity switch that *A Tale of Two Cities*' Sidney Carton, who took another's place at the guillotine, would have understood and approved? The compelling evidence – and reading it defies you not to cheer – is that Horrie lived to fight and play another day and make love on many another night.

'He was whisked away to northern Victoria, where he lived out his days and sired many puppies,' Anthony Hill revealed in his book on animals who served with Australian forces, *Animal Heroes* (2005).

This new and improved happy ending to the story of the little dog now makes it suitable for a Hollywood feature film. Hugh Jackman could be cast in the supporting role of Horrie's master, Jim, and as Horrie . . . well, you could cast just about any Jack

Russell with the head of the proverbial robber's dog: a Russell Crowe–type dog.

Horrie wasn't a robber's dog, as far as it's known. But he wasn't pretty. He was just a mongrel, a little runt of a dog with a big heart beating under his skinny ribs who saw action in some of the darkest days of World War II. In Egypt, he trained with the Australian Infantry Force's 2/1st Australian Machine Gun Battalion for the campaigns to come. In Greece, Horrie and his mates were relentlessly bombed by the invading Germans. In Crete, he was wounded when his ship went down. In Syria, he fought French troops who had gone over to the Germans. Through it all, Horrie's courage and fighting spirit never deserted him. He never wavered in his devotion to his mates. And in turn they were there when Horrie desperately needed them.

Horrie joined the AIF in Egypt in 1942 when Jim Moody and Don Gill, a couple of Aussie privates stationed in the Western Desert, noticed a pup chasing lizards among the rocks. He was hopping with fleas and rather comical looking with stumpy legs, a long body and not much of a tail to wag. But he was clearly in need of a good feed and Jim tucked him under his arm and took him back to the camp. He was, they reckoned, an Arab dog who had survived cruel treatment: he would bark furiously if Arabs came near the camp.

Within a week, Horrie the Wog Dog, as they called him, was everybody's mate, and a valued member of the battalion. No route march could start until Horrie was in the vanguard. The little dog took his place at the head of the column and proudly led it out. At night he guarded the camp against thieves. He was given a promotion, he was now Corporal Horrie, and wore a uniform, a khaki coat cut down from a regular army issue and complete with corporal ensigns.

Then, without notice, the days of training and route marches were over as the battalion was rushed to Greece to help stem the

German invasion. Horrie went too. It was against regulations, but by now Jim had trained him to travel, keeping still and quiet, in his kitbag. Seasick on the way over, like many another Digger, Horrie was ready for action when he and his mates arrived in Athens. They were just in time to join what was to become one of the most disastrous retreats of the war. Day after day, the Luftwaffe were bombing and machine-gunning the retreating Allied columns. Horrie became an air-raid siren – the best. When the little dog suddenly sat to attention, his ears cocked, the men of the machine gun battalion knew he was hearing enemy planes on their way. Then Horrie's frenzied barking alerted the troops down the line to the imminent attack. British Tommies, Kiwis, Greeks, Yugoslavs and Australians scrambled off and away from the truck convoy and when the Stukas roared overhead the men had whatever cover they could find. Horrie saved hundreds of Allied troops. At night Horrie was on sentry duty, alert for saboteurs, as he had been in Egypt.

They were evacuated from Greece by night just as the Germans were about to invade. Horrie's ship, the *Costa Rica*, was hit by a torpedo and sunk, but Moody held Horrie close and he and his mates jumped from it to the destroyer *Defender* that had swung alongside to their rescue. They were taken to Crete where Horrie was given new orders. He became a messenger. Men on patrol would tie despatches in a handkerchief around Horrie's collar and he'd race back to deliver them to Moody.

Once again they were ordered to be evacuated, this time back to Egypt, and once again the bombing was almost non-stop. Horrie was hit in the shoulder by a sliver of shrapnel and as Moody and Gill dug it out the little dog never whimpered.

In Tel Aviv, waiting to be shipped back to Australia and then to be sent to fight the Japanese in New Guinea, Moody and Gill took their mate to a vet. They'd been through a lot together and they had no intention of leaving him behind. The vet kept the little dog for a week, put him through tests and gave him a clean bill of health.

Now it was a matter of smuggling Horrie on to the boat to Australia. Moody had long before cut a hole in the back of his kitbag for Horrie to quickly pop into on command. When Moody had the pack on his back he'd wet his finger in his water bottle and Horrie would lick it through a ventilation hole. That was how Horrie boarded the ship. It was a risky business – a cat and a dog, smuggled aboard had been discovered and peremptorily thrown overboard. Moody was much more careful with Horrie. He was kept in a cabin where someone was with him at all times, and if there was a knock on the door Horrie would jump into his smuggler's pack and his companion would toss some clothes over it.

He went ashore when the ship docked in Adelaide and from there was sent to Melbourne to live with Henry Moody, Jim's dad, until Jim got back from New Guinea.

And there the story should end, with Horrie living happily every after, an old soldier never dying, just fading away. Instead, three years after he had come into Australia, he was ordered to be put down. Horrie, said an officious bureaucracy, was an illegal immigrant who had evaded quarantine. He must be 'destroyed'.

Horrie's existence had been discovered when the Commonwealth Director of Veterinary Hygiene, Mr RN Wardle, saw an article about Horrie and how Jim had smuggled him into Australia. Mr RN Wardle saw red. He ordered his officers to seize Horrie. Jim Moody and Horrie were staying at Don Gill's Sydney home when the officials tracked them down, and Jim, distressed, asked them to give him one more week with his old mate.

A week later the officers returned for Horrie. They waited while Jim said a sad farewell, took the little dog, and, at 4 pm on Monday 12 March, gave him a dose of cyanide.

Horrie's death was front-page news. The nation was outraged.

How Horrie the Wog Dog Fooled Us All

Public meetings, questions in Parliament, the Prime Minister under fire, editorials thundering, abusive letters flooding in to Mr RN Wardle's office, a wreath was at the Cenotaph – all in vain. Horrie was gone.

But was he?

Canberra author Anthony Hill thought he was familiar with the story of Horrie until a friend suggested that he write a book about the gallant little dog. He picks up the story in the preface to *Animal Heroes*.

> 'But Ion Idriess wrote that book in 1945,' I said. 'Horrie was destroyed by the quarantine authorities three years after he got here.'
>
> 'I mean,' Norma replied, 'that you should say what really happened.'
>
> And for the first time in nearly 60 years, she broke her silence and told me the tale of the substitute dog – as Horrie's owner, Jim Moody, had told it to her ... I was able to confirm the main details of the story with two of Jim's children, Ian and Leonie Moody, and also with Brian and Betty Featherstone. Brian is probably the last surviving member of the signal platoon 'Rebels' of 2/1 Machine Gun Battalion ... Through them I learnt how Jim had the last laugh on bureaucratic authority: of the switch, and of the 'five bob dog.' He was a Horrie look-alike, who was bought for five shillings from a Sydney pound and given to the officials when they demanded Jim hand over his dog for destruction.

Jim Moody was saddened to hand over the substitute look-alike dog he had found and bought for five shillings at the pound. But the sacrifice of the unwanted little dog, doomed in any case, allowed Horrie to happily live the rest of his life on a farm in northern Victoria.

Horrie's memorabilia is on exhibit at the Australian War Memorial in Canberra. There is Jim's ventilated kitbag, Horrie's khaki 'corporal's' jacket and his campaign medals. And up and down the east coast of Australia there are hundreds of little Horries and Horriettas, whose ancestor was the courageous little dog the Nazis and the bureaucrats couldn't kill.

FRANCIS DE GROOT and the Day He Saw Red

Francis Edward de Groot wanted to see the back of 'the Big Fella', the firebrand New South Wales Premier, Jack Lang. He despised him. Lang, he knew, was not a communist – Lang hated communism – but he was certainly a dangerous socialist. So that Saturday morning, on the Sydney Harbour Bridge, when de Groot did see the hulking back of 'the Big Fella' – a daunting 193 centimetres and 100 kilograms – he saw red in more ways than one.

'I applied both spurs, shaking up my poor old horse in a way that he had probably not experienced in years.' Drawing a sword, de Groot slashed the ceremonial ribbon on the Sydney Harbour Bridge, declaring the bridge open 'in the name of the decent and respectable people of New South Wales'.

It was not the opening Australia had been waiting for.

At its beginning in 1925, the bridge was going to cost the astronomical sum of 4,217,721 pounds, 11 shillings and 10 pence. It would span Sydney Harbour from Dawes Point in the city, where the first settlers had established the infant colony, to Milson's Point on the northern shore. It was the largest and heaviest steel arch bridge ever built; its two cantilevered half arches, anchored by 128 immense wire cables would reach over the water until they came almost close enough to touch, less than a metre apart. Then a long pilot pin would be inserted between them, the cables would be gradually slackened and the two halves would meet as one. The riveters would then seal the marriage of 650,000 tonnes of steel.

Beneath the arch, 440 feet high, gigantic girders would hang to support the two-way rail tracks and the eight-lane roadway below. And on the roadway, the bridge would be officially opened sometime in the coming decade.

It took eight years, cost double the initial budget and claimed the lives of 16 workers, but on 19 March 1932, the splendid Sydney Harbour Bridge, our first national monument, was ready.

So too was Francis de Groot.

Born in Dublin in 1883, de Groot served with distinction in World War I, enlisting in the 15th Hussars and finishing in the 15th Tank Battalion with the rank of acting captain and this prescient report from his commander: 'Excellent disciplinarian and leader of men, a very determined officer with plenty of dash.'

After the war the Irishman and his wife Bessie came to Sydney where he opened a successful business making reproduction furniture of high quality. He also got involved in the political turmoil that gripped Sydney and Melbourne.

In 1932, the height of the Great Depression, communism and paramilitary organisations – in Sydney called the Old Guard and its offshoot the New Guard, mostly made up of veterans of the war organised into ranks and divisions, and armed – clashed often. Loyalty to the British Throne and support for the British Empire was at the core of the New Guard's platform along with the suppression of disloyal or immoral elements in government, industry and society. De Groot, a 'zone commander' in the New Guard, was an ardent Empire loyalist who like all the New Guard saw the Premier, Jack Lang, as a disloyal radical leading the state to ruin.

Lang, a bellicose bully who revelled in his harsh Australian accent and enjoyed ruffling the feathers of the Establishment, presided over a state with 31 per cent unemployment, street battles in Sydney between communists and conservatives, and a huge debt to British bondholders. Lang announced that interest payments to these bondholders should not be paid, an act the New Guard considered treason. The Federal Government responded to this by drafting legislation, the *Financial Agreements Enforcement Bill,* to allow the Treasurer to seize NSW's money and use it to pay the outstanding interest. Lang's answer to that was typical of the man.

On Saturday morning, 12 March 1932, the day the legislation would become law, and a week before he was due to open the Harbour Bridge, Lang sent treasury officials with suitcases and accompanied by armed police to two banks. At the Commonwealth Bank the men withdrew £400,000 in small denominations and packed it in the suitcases. At the Bank of NSW they took away £750,000. At noon the legislation became law. Too late. The bank account of the state of NSW now showed £0-0-0.

The New Guard was outraged. Plots were hatched to destroy Lang – beginning with stopping him from opening the bridge the following Saturday. The founder of the New Guard, Eric Campbell, a shrill and bombastic solicitor who had served with the Australian Imperial Force, announced publicly that the New Guard would prevent the Premier opening the bridge. How the New Guard would do that Campbell didn't divulge. In fact, he didn't know.

'As the big day drew near,' de Groot wrote, 'a number of the young hotheads were not satisfied with vague promises and I commenced to hear all kinds of harebrained schemes, such as plots to kidnap Mr Lang, and some of the boys were quite capable of it too; also I would not have given much for his chances of survival if they had laid hands on him.'

A few days before the ceremony, however, the fortuitous

publication of the popular magazine *Smith's Weekly* inspired a new way to 'get' the Big Fella.

One of the magazine's artists, Nils Jorset 'Joe' Jonsson, came up with a cartoon that paid homage to HM Bateman's famous series of cartoons, 'The man who . . .' These cartoons invariably depicted a 'little man' inadvertently causing consternation in the ranks of the pompous upper class by an innocent action.

Jonsson's cartoon, captioned, 'The man who beat Lang to the tape' had an everyday Sydneysider slashing the ceremonial ribbon while Lang and the VIPs staggered back, aghast. The cartoon delighted the New Guard; kidnapping was off the agenda. Now it knew what to do.

De Groot was deputed to be the man who beat Lang to the tape. He got his Hussars uniform out of mothballs, buffed his ceremonial sword and borrowed a horse, Mick, a 16.5-hand chestnut. On the following Saturday morning, he joined Lang, the Governor General, the NSW Governor, state premiers, generals and admirals, a surfeit of sundry VIPs, dozens of top-hatted dignitaries, assorted alderman and, it seemed, almost all of Sydney's million-and-a-quarter citizens on the bridge. They were there for the ceremony, 'that every Sydneysider had waited seven years to see,' de Groot wrote, 'the opening of the bridge we had all watched creep across the harbour from each side.'

The Big Fella had announced he would do the honours. No need for the Governor, Sir Philip Game, to bother himself cutting a ribbon. And he would do it dressed as he always was in public: in a black homburg hat and a three-piece lounge suit. No need to go to the expense of buying top-hat and tails.

At 10 am, de Groot arrived on the bridge. Mounted on Mick, in his uniform and with his gleaming sword in its scabbard, he was presumed to be part of the official ceremonies. 'It was a perfect March day, even for Sydney,' de Groot wrote. 'I wondered, should I do anything about it or just sit there and enjoy the show, later

Field Marshal Blamey with Prime Minister John Curtin pictured during the struggle to defeat the Japanese in Papua New Guinea. Blamey, the supreme commander of Australia's forces was given the rank of Field Marshal in his dying days but he never commanded the respect of most who served under him.
© *Newspix*

Alan Bond, flying high and laughing all the way to the bank... before the $825 million nosedive.
© *Newspix*

Al Grassby, more decorously dressed than usual, poses before the Australian flag. His real loyalty was to the murderers of Donald Mackay.
Michael Jones © Newspix

Marcus Einfeld leaves court to begin his jail sentence: a Living Legend, brought down by a puny traffic penalty.
Troy Bendeich © Newspix

Andrew Scott, the self-styled Captain Moonlite, perhaps grieved at being outshone by Ned Kelly, took a bunch of five feckless young men to Wantabadgery, near Wagga Wagga (below).
Police Records Victoria Collection

There 300 spectators sat down to watch and cheer the police siege. Two men died in the shootout and Scott and another went to the gallows.
Wood engraving from the Australasian Sketcher

Daisy Bates and Breaker Morant came to Queensland the same year, met, married and separated almost at once and went on to become unique figures in our history. Daisy was renowned throughout the British Empire for her work with Aborigines, and the Breaker's legacy was inspired by his reputed last words in front of a firing squad.

Both successfully masqueraded as high born. The reality was somewhat more mundane.
© *Newspix*

Wilfred Burchett won fame for his exclusive report on Hiroshima in the aftermath of the Atom Bomb. In the post-war years, the Cold War, he became a 'Fellow Traveller' favourably reporting, always, on the side of the USSR. During the Korean War he actively sided with the Chinese in the interrogation of UN Prisoners-of-War.
© *Newspix*

Les Kane (left) and Ray Bennett had once been friends. The friendship ended when Bennett, the mastermind of the Great Bookie Robbery, with two others, waited for Kane to come home, shut family out of sight and machine gunned him. Kane's brother then shot Bennett dead in the Melbourne Magistrates Court.
© *Newspix*

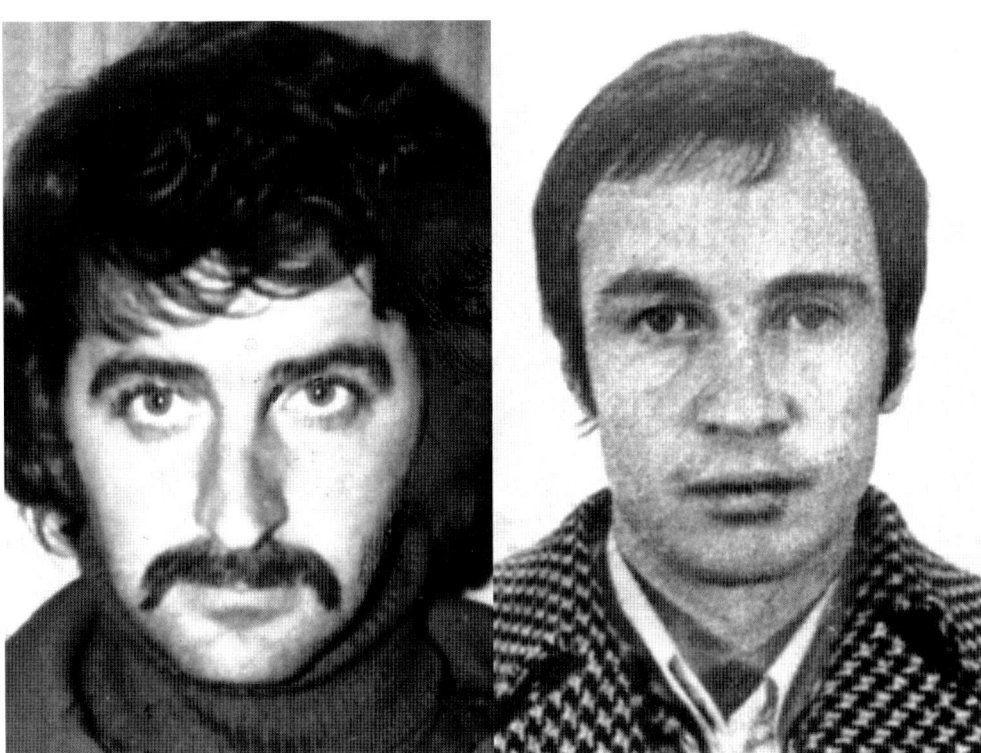

If any publicity is good publicity, the scandal that engulfed Melbourne's triumphant rugby league team was the perfect publicity storm.

Peter Foster in Fiji, where he was to be arrested, swimming for freedom in his underpants. A master salesman, his liaison with buxom Samantha Fox and his later business association with Cherie Blair, the wife of the then UK prime minister, made him, he says, an 'international man of mystery'.
© *Newspix*

Frank Hardy invented a history of his father and the Hardy family struggling to survive during the Depression. Undoubtedly Hardy meant to portray himself as a 'worker' dedicated to the cause of communism. His defamation of the wife of the millionaire John Wren was similarly in the cause of 'The Party'.
© *Newspix*

TE Lawrence, dramatically lit and posing in the garb of an Arab prince falsely claimed the credit that belonged to Harry Chauvel (above) and the Australian Light Horse, seen (below) entering Jerusalem. Lawrence mixed with the greats and pretended to shun the spotlight but assiduously built the myth of Lawrence of Arabia.
Newspix (Chauvel) / Imperial War Museum (TE Lawrence) / Australian War Memorial B01619 (Light Horse entering Jerusalem)

Trainer Hayden Haitana with the ring-in 'Fine Cotton'. Seen below winning the minor race that will be remembered long after most Melbourne Cup champions are forgotten, Fine Cotton's name is secure in racing lore. The almost hilarious mishaps that accompanied the inept ring-in, however, obscured a darker story.
© *Newspix*

Jim Cairns, the Treasurer of Australia, with Juni Morosi in tow. A faint whiff of a caveman and his conquest, the image was one of a series of damaging blows to the Labor Government of Gough Whitlam.
© *Newspix*

Francis De Groot in the moment he slashed at the ceremonial ribbons and declared the Sydney Harbour Bridge open 'in the name of the people of New South Wales'.
© *Newspix*

The Sun News-Pictorial's front page report on De Groot's unofficial and unorthodox opening of the bridge. The paper's use of photographs, radical in its time, made it, as it still is, the top-selling daily in the nation.
© Newspix

On the beach at Anzac Cove, seen here shortly after the landing at Gallipoli. The Gallipoli debacle cost the lives of 8700 Australians. But when they left Anzac Cove, in a brilliantly devised retreat that had the Turks believing the Australians were still in the trenches and still firing, the Anzac legend was complete.
Australian War Memorial

England's captain Mike Gatting, totally bewildered, as Shane Warne rattles his stumps. First ball in England, First Test, Warne's 'Ball of the Century,' introduced him to the English, a shock from which they still haven't recovered.
© *Newspix*

Max Harris, the young and brilliant publisher of the avant garde magazine *Angry Penguins* instantly fell for the concocted story of the tormented poet, Ern Malley. Malley, he was convinced, was tragically taken before his time like so many other precocious poetic geniuses.
© *Newspix*

Murderous Len Lawson, the picture of a sedate and assured artist, with his portrait of the Catholic Archbishop Mannix. Lawson was the creator of the Lone Avenger, seen on the front cover of this book – an Australian hero to a generation of schoolboys, a cartoon character every bit as good as the Lone Ranger, who he resembled in more ways than one.

Carnival hand Rupert Stuart, in custody and facing execution for the rape and murder of a young girl. Rupert Murdoch's campaign to re-examine the evidence that led to his conviction – particularly the confession he was said to have dictated – almost led to Murdoch being charged with treason. But it saved Stuart.
© *Newspix*

Left, Murdoch in Fleet Street sees his new paper, *The Sun*, come hot off the presses.
© *Newspix*

Ned Kelly, photographed the day before he was hanged. Kelly had argued that he should not be tried for murder, 'I was compelled to shoot them or lie down and let them shoot me,' but the judge – wrongly – ruled that the jury could not consider a verdict of manslaughter.
Victorian Police Historical Unit

Above right: Horrie, the dog that fooled a nation.

Right: Lindy and Michael Chamberlain's seemingly detached demeanour, misled most Australians to believe that their daughter Azaria had not been taken by a dingo, but had been murdered.

Gough Whitlam, head high, half listens as his Dismissal is formally read on the steps of Parliament. At its conclusion, 'God save the Queen,' Whitlam pronounced his famous rejoinder: 'Well may he say God save the Queen, because nothing will save the Governor-General!' Whitlam may have been composing this famous quote as the Dismissal was read.

The murder of Alma Tirtschke, seen here with her mother and little sister, was not killed by Colin Ross (right). He hanged for her murder, nonetheless. In 2010 he was posthumously pardoned by the Victorian Government – but Ross was not, as he should have been, reprieved.

WHO SAW THIS CHILD?

going home quietly . . . In spite of my strong feelings against Mr Lang's regime, I might have let him get away with it only for one factor that had quite decided me. A few minutes before, when the Governor-General had arrived, the RAA Band had played the national anthem.'

At the strains of *God Save the Queen,* de Groot and most of the men on the bridge bared their heads. 'But not the premier of the state, Mr Lang. He remained covered, and, taking their cue from him, the majority of the men in the stands nearest to me. Not only kept their hats on but laughed and jeered at those who did uncover. I no longer had any doubts.'

He dug his heels into Mick's flanks, urged the horse forward and drew his sword. When he reached the ribbons the horse reared in fright, and de Groot slashed at them, gashing but not severing them. Then he stooped, grabbed the ribbons, and as they broke apart shouted, 'I declare this bridge open in the name of the decent and respectable people of New South Wales.'

It might be imagined that de Groot's audacious unofficial opening would have left the Big Fella stunned, his eyes popping and his great prognathous jaw hanging open. But late in his life Lang claimed that he had missed the fun. He was, he said, 'about 600 yards away on the official platform with hundreds of people around me'. This would seem to contradict de Groot's account that he had been incensed by Lang failing to doff his Homburg hat, a difficult thing to see half a mile away. 'Anyway it's all of no consequence,' Lang said. 'All I know is that I cut the ribbon again later and opened the bridge.'

If Lang did indeed miss the incident, he certainly didn't want anyone else to see it. A Cinesound cameraman, possibly Ken Hall, was on the spot, had spoken to de Groot asking him to move his horse for a better camera angle, and had captured the dramatic moment on film. Lang banned the film from being shown in cinemas. In the intervening decades the film and the image of de Groot slashing at the ribbons has been screened and reproduced countless times, no doubt to the chagrin of the Big Fella.

Eight months after his short ride into history, de Groot and the New Guard explored the possibility of going over with 'a considerable number of men' to link with the Melbourne paramilitary League of National Security, another secret organisation, possibly headed by Victoria's Chief Commissioner of Police, Major General Thomas Blamey.

In 1950, de Groot and his wife went back to Ireland, where he died in 1969.

Jack Lang lasted another two tumultuous months in office. He had instructed public servants not to pay money into the Federal Treasury and the Governor Sir Philip Game deemed that illegal. On 13 May he sacked Lang – the first of only two dismissals in Australian history. The Big Fella went with a brave face. 'I am no longer Premier but a free man,' he said.

It was as well he did. On the evening of his dismissal a brigade of hundreds of New Guard men waited in the basement of a department store near Parliament House. They were ready to march on Parliament House if he did not resign before 7 o'clock. Lang went at 6 o'clock. And at the state elections the following month Lang Labor seats fell from 55 to 24.

Lang survived de Groot by six years. In his last years he had become a cult figure to some and a mentor for the young Paul Keating, who may have inherited his contempt for Conservatives and the British upper class from the Big Fella. Years later, when Prime Minster Keating outraged the British media by daring to touch the Queen was he, on behalf of the Big Fella, subconsciously turning the tables on the ghost of Francis de Groot?

MURDOCH's Wapping War

Fleet Street newspapers are produced in conditions which combine a protection racket with a lunatic asylum.
— Columnist Bernard Levin in the *Times*

Rupert Murdoch moved into the street in 1969 and his neighbours looked down their nose.

The Fleet Street newcomer was a colonial, an Australian. He apparently owned a rag in Sydney and another, very small-potatoes newspaper in Adelaide, wherever that was. Now he was trying to make his mark in Fleet Street, buying a moribund broadsheet, the *Sun*, and bringing in his Aussie journo mates and a cartoonist named Rigby to show the English-speaking-world's finest newspapers how it was done.

He wore a cat-that-swallowed-the-canary grin. No-one was quite sure why, but everyone agreed that the situation was too comical and the betting was that he'd be sent back to the colonies, cleaned out, within a year.

But then Murdoch bought a Fleet Street institution, the *News of the World,* and the owners of the Street's newspapers – the *Mirror*, the *Daily Mail*, the *Sketch*, the *Evening News*, the *Evening Standard*, the *Daily Express*, the *Daily Telegraph*, the *Times*, the *Observer*, the *Financial Times* and more – were not amused. The *News of the World,* or the 'News of the Screws' as it was irreverently known, specialised in salacious gossip. Its reporters were forever finding themselves in sleazy situations that inevitably ended with them extricating themselves before things got too X-rated. These stories always concluded: 'I made an excuse and then left,' and were often accompanied by 'shocking' front-page photographs with a 'pointer' that promised: More shocking photos inside!' Nevertheless, the 'Screws' was an institution, not meant for the likes of the Australian intruder.

Murdoch's acquisition of the *News of the World,* brilliantly plucked from the grasp of the crooked Robert Maxwell and for a pittance, sent a shiver up the rival proprietors' pusillanimous spines. 'The Dirty Digger', as *Private Eye* dubbed him, was in town to stay and already he had shown acumen for every aspect of bringing out a successful newspaper. Though the elite Left magazine the *New Statesman* had dubbed the *Sun* the 'shit sheet', Murdoch had doubled its circulation within a year, taking almost all of it from the market leader, the *Mirror*. Murdoch was showing them all how it was done. From finding the story, writing and subediting it, setting it, printing it and getting the newspapers on to the trucks and away, Murdoch understood it all because he'd done it all. Now he was revealing a new trick: a terrifying grasp of the technique of takeovers. And the cat-that-swallowed-the-canary grin was widening.

In the seventies he moved into the US, once again starting small and rapidly elbowing his way into the front ranks. In 1976 he bought the *New York Post*. Five years later he returned to Fleet Street to win control of the most sacred of all British newspapers, the *Times* and the *Sunday Times*. In the mid-eighties he bought the *Boston Herald* and the *Chicago Sun-Times* and – crucially – Twentieth Century-Fox film studios and Metromedia, a chain of television stations. The film studios and the television stations gave Murdoch the opportunity to establish a fourth national television network in the US – Fox Broadcasting.

But in 1986, faced with debts mounting from his acquisitions in the US, Murdoch initiated a revolution in an industry that had stubbornly resisted almost all and any attempts to modernise it. For six years Murdoch had tried to persuade the print unions to agree to move into a new £100 million printing plant in the old east London docklands area of Wapping. That, originally, was all it was intended for: printing. And for six years the unions insisted that they would not go unless they could import the ludicrous restrictive practices that by now were now crippling some of Fleet Street's most famous newspapers.

Rupert Murdoch picks up the story, in a 1989 speech he gave in New York for the Manhattan Institute:

> Incredibly, as recently as four years ago, British newspapers were still printed with hot lead, a process that had changed only by degrees since Gutenberg's day. British labour unions had successfully prevented the technological revolution from reaching Fleet Street. They had a noose around the neck of the industry, and they pulled it very tight.
>
> In 1986, we had to hire four men to run a printing press in San Antonio, Texas. In Chicago, it took a maximum of five men; in New York and Sydney, six. In London, it took 18 men to do the same job, all paid salaries at least 100 percent above the national average.
>
> Eighteen men could not even get near a printing press at the same time. But they were not expected to. They were paid fulltime for working half-shifts, sometimes only on alternate days, occasionally only once every three weeks. Many of our employees worked second jobs – 90 per cent of the *News of the World* publishing department, for example. Some worked for rival publications, some were cab drivers or mechanics, one owned a vineyard, another was a mortician.

Once we found that phone calls to the *Sun* were not being answered because the switchboard team was watching Wimbledon on television. When asked to stop (or at least turn down the sound), they threatened 'industrial action'. Another night, a big news story broke in the US, but failed to reach the *Sun* press room because our telex operator, surrounded by yards of copy churning out of the machine, was asleep. We complained, but in the end we had to apologize for disturbing him.

Naturally, we got pretty tired of this kind of thing.

Murdoch decided to break the print unions' stranglehold on production. He had two options. If the unions allowed him to print some of the *Sun* and the *News of the World* at Wapping he would use the rest of the plant to print a new paper, the *London Post*. The second option, if the unions wouldn't agree to this, was the Big Bang: he would produce *all* his newspapers at Wapping.

The unions suspected that the *London Post* was nothing more than a gambit, and negotiations got nowhere. Telephone calls to them went unanswered. Murdoch, meanwhile, in cloak-and-dagger secrecy at what was to become known as Fortress Wapping, began installing computers from the U.S., printers from Australia, and truckers from outside London, and began planning how to print and distribute News Corp's 35 million newspapers a week from there.

In March 1985, News Corp announced that it would be printing the *London Post* at Wapping. Days later, on the *Sun*, a printing plate broke, one of 60 breaks in the previous two years. It started an 11-day strike. In the past this would have been enough to bring the newspaper owners to their knees, grovelling to be allowed to give the unions more power and more money. Not this time. Throughout the latter half of 1985, in the huge printing hall at

Wapping, the computers, the presses, the ink, the paper, all were quietly brought in under cover. By 1986, with the unions still being bloody minded and aggressive – and foolishly believing that they were being bluffed – the Big Bang was ready to go off.

Murdoch told the Manhattan Institute:

> This was what you might call 'betting the company'. Fleet Street unions had not lost a fight in living memory. But we were encouraged by Mrs Thatcher's victory in the miners' strike and by signs that authorities were prepared to protect private property from the actions of massed pickets. The London police were not necessarily on our side. One morning, they even threatened to arrest the editor of the *Sun* for making an impolite gesture at the pickets. But sympathetic or unsympathetic, the police would not let the picketers block our trucks. An appalling number of officers were injured during the Battle of Wapping; on one night, after 300 mounted police faced 11,000 demonstrators, 162 officers (and 33 demonstrators) were injured. But the trucks rolled. And in the end we won.
>
> The immediate result of our victory was greater freedom and flexibility, and higher profits, for News Corp. But the Battle of Wapping also ushered in a silver age of British newspaper journalism. Suddenly, thanks to the new technology, it became a lot cheaper to start a newspaper. The result is that, since 1986, a number of completely new national newspapers have sprouted up. Now of course, we did not fight the Battle of Wapping because we wanted to bring a silver age to British journalism. When the beaver gnaws down a tree, he is not thinking of his vital ecological role either. Nevertheless, he has one.

Murdoch offered the unions redundancy payments of £50 million although he was not obliged to do so. The unions were on strike.

They turned down the money, leading Murdoch to say they now had 'no jobs, no recognition, and now no money'.

Rupert Murdoch deceived the unions. But the Battle of Wapping saved the British newspaper industry. If not for Wapping the restrictive practices, the frivolous strikes and the cowardly management which always caved in to the unions, would have driven all but a handful of newspapers – possibly owned by Murdoch's News Corporation – to the wall.

Could the war been avoided? Andrew Neil, the editor of the *Sunday Times* during the Wapping war, wrote in 2006 in the *Observer*.

> For 13 months my life was blighted by physical attacks, death threats, bodyguards everywhere I went and 5000 screaming, violent pickets at the doorstep of my office every Saturday night, nobody would have benefited more than me from doing it differently . . .
>
> At one stage, a union official hurled a box of matches across the table at us, shouting: 'Why don't you just burn the place down? Don't you understand? We're never going to go there!' If we'd taken his advice, not just Wapping but the British newspaper business would have gone down in flames.

GALLIPOLI and the Triumphant Retreat

'The finest body of young men ever brought together in modern times,' John Masefield, England's Poet Laureate, wrote of the Anzacs. 'For physical beauty and ability of bearing, they surpassed any man I have ever seen.' To this unqualified adulation others completed the portrait. The Anzacs, they wrote, were recklessly courageous and resourceful; men who stuck by their mates, scorned authority and never lost their laconic, larrikin sense of humour.

That is the Anzac legend. But is it a myth?

The remarkable fact is that most of it is true and that almost a century after it was created the unique Anzac spirit is still alive and honoured.

The central storyteller of the spirit that was summed up in the acronym ANZACS – Australian and New Zealand Army Corps – was Australia's official war correspondent, Captain C.E.W. (Charles) Bean. But it was an English journalist's newspaper report, the first account Australians read of the landing at Gallipoli, that riveted the nation and overnight sowed the seeds of the Anzac legend.

Les Carlyon, in his definitive account of the Dardanelles campaign, *Gallipoli*, says Ellis Ashmead-Bartlett 'was a journalist-adventurer, the sort of man who once made Fleet Street interesting, and he knew about war. He had served in the Boer

War as a Lieutenant, and reported at least seven others, several of them involving Turkey. He was the sort of man who could write "Hire of yak – £500" on an expense claim and not blush.'

Reporting from the bridge of the battleship *London*, Ashmead-Bartlett, was able to take in the entire sweep of the landing on the Anzac beachhead. Then he joined the troops. Newspapers around Australia carried the sensational news on 30 April.

Its impact was immediate. Aside from the thrilling account of the battle, Ashmead-Bartlett's admiration for the Australians was astounding. It revealed to those at home, C.P. Smith of the Melbourne *Argus* wrote, 'that our men were giants, a new strange race that had no fear, and who could face almost certain death as if they sought to die. Only then did we understand what splendid fellows these were, and what a proud thing it was to be Australian.'

This is an edited account of that report:

By 1 o'clock in the morning [of April 25] the ships had reached the rendezvous, five miles from the appointed landing place, and the soldiers were roused and served with the last hot meal.

The Australians, who were about to go into action for the first time in trying circumstances, were cheerful, quiet, and confident. There was no sign of nerves nor of excitement.

As the moon waned, the boats were swung out, the Australians received their last instructions, and men who six months ago had been living peaceful civilian lives had begun to disembark on a strange and unknown shore in a strange land to attack an enemy of a different race . . .

The work of disembarking proceeded mechanically under a point blank fire. The moment the boats touched the beach the troops jumped ashore and doubled for cover, but the gallant boat crews had to pull in and out under the galling fire from hundreds of points.

. . . The Australians rose to the occasion. Not waiting for

orders, or for the boats to reach the beach, they sprang into the sea, and, forming a sort of rough line, rushed at the enemy's trenches.

Their magazines were not charged, so they just went in with cold steel.

It was over in a minute. The Turks in the first trench were either bayoneted or they ran away, and their Maxim was captured.

Then the Australians found themselves facing an almost perpendicular cliff of loose sandstone, covered with thick shrubbery. Somewhere, about half-way up, the enemy had a second trench, strongly held, from which they poured a terrible fire on the troops below and the boats pulling back to the destroyers for the second landing party.

Ashmead-Bartlett's enthusiasm didn't stop at those men storming the heights.

> ... I have never seen anything like these wounded Australians in war before.
> Though many were shot to bits, without the hope of recovery, their cheers resounded throughout the night ... They were happy because they knew that they had been used for the first time and had not been found wanting.

Bursting with pride at this first news of glorious valour, Australia, within a week, was reeling at the reality of the landing. By then, of 23,292 Anzacs who had landed on the beach, some 5000 Australians were dead or wounded. In cities and country towns, the grieving began.

There was to be another eight months of slaughter before the Anzacs left Gallipoli. And in that time the legend was nourished by the reports of bands of brave men in ferocious hand-to-hand battles, and of individual heroes like Simpson and his donkey, and Captain Albert Jacka, VC. But the truth of the most horrific chapter of the Anzacs' Gallipoli story, the carnage – murder, it was later called – of the vital strategic point known as the Nek was never told. The senseless slaughter was the climax of Peter Weir's 1981 film *Gallipoli*. '... so well done that for many it is the reference point on the Gallipoli campaign,' Les Carlyon wrote. 'Yet its final scenes, built around the fourth charge at the Nek, are inaccurate and unfair to the British. The film suggests the Australians at the Nek were being sacrificed to help the landing at Suvla. It also suggests that a British officer was ordering successive waves of Australians to run out and commit suicide.

'The scale of the tragedy of the Nek was mostly the work of two Australian incompetents, Hughes and Antill. Hughes was the brigade commander and he didn't command. Antill wasn't the brigade commander and he did.'

Australia's prime minister, 'Billy' Hughes, burnished the legend in this speech but ignored the culpability of the commanders at the Nek:

> The story of how the 8th Light Horse of Australia went out to die in the dark hour before the dawn, when the tides of life are at their ebb, is one by which even that of the Charge of the Light Brigade must pale its fires.
>
> There were some 500 of them, and they were to attack in three waves. They were given their orders six, eight, 10 hours before. Every man believed that he was going out to almost certain death. Yet they did not hesitate. They made their preparations. They handed to those who were to remain in the trench their poor brief messages of farewell, and waited calmly for the order.
>
> In the dark hour when night is yielding doggedly to day, these young soldiers of Australia went out to die. As the blast of

the whistle sounded, the first wave leaped from the trench, but nearly all fell back dead upon their fellows who were waiting their turn in the trench. None got more than a few yards before being shot down. In the face of this awful sight the second line, undaunted, leaped out. Of these only five or six remained on their feet after they had gone 10 or 12 yards. The third wave followed in their turn and met the same fate. The wounded lay exposed to the pitiless machine-gun fire of the Turks, which poured a veritable hail of death into their poor, bleeding bodies. The colonel was killed at the head of his men 50 yards from the trench. Eighteen officers went out – two only returned. Of the men the merest handful survived.

We must look back into the grey dawn of history before we find a deed parallel with this. The Spartans of Thermopylæ have left an imperishable name, whose glory has shone through the ages with a lustre which time has not dimmed and which will burn brightly when the pyramids have crumbled to dust and the proudest monuments of kings are no more. But surely what these young Australian soldiers did that day – these men of a new nation, the last but one in the family of the great British Empire – what these men did, too, will live for ever!

Gallipoli cost 8700 Australians lives. But the sense of the Anzacs being at one with the heroes of ancient Greece was underpinned at the conclusion of the tragedy. The evacuation of Gallipoli on 19 December was done in so masterly a fashion that it became an intrinsic part of the legend: the Trojan horse in reverse. The Turks were completely deceived by a brilliant strategy designed to convince them that the Anzacs were, as always, at their posts and firing.

There were only two minor casualties where there might have been a massacre. And the Anzacs left laconically. 'You didn't push us off, Jacko, we just left', one Australian wrote in a note left for the Turks. Strictly speaking that was incorrect. But that was the Anzac spirit.

This is an edited extract from CEW Bean's hour-by-hour report of the evacuation, filed for the *Sydney Morning Herald*.

> Three miles away from me, across a grey, silky sea, lies the dark shape of the land. Eight months ago, just as the first lemon-grey of dawn was breaking over that long, lizard-shaped mountain, I watched such signs as were visible of the landing of the Australian troops in Gallipoli. Now, as the night falls gradually down upon the same historic spot, I am watching for the signs of their departure.
>
> For tonight the first and second divisions are leaving the old position of Anzac. The New Zealand and Australian division is leaving the slopes and foothills of the range. Further north, the Indian Brigade is leaving Hill 60, where for months it has overlooked Suvla flats. And further north still from across those same flats, with the chocolate hill in the middle of them, and in the distance the slopes of Kirecteh Tepe, the British are retiring from the position which the world knows as Suvla.
>
> All the non-essential corps were sent away during the previous week. Night after night on the beach, one found trooping by along covered routes down to the piers, ambulances, hospitals, engineers, army service corps – all the men, in fact, except those actually carrying rifles.
>
> The moon is just beginning to flood sea and land with a light so clear that you can scarcely notice the change from twilight into night. This brightness of the moon is one of our chief anxieties, for if the enemy sees what we are doing and attacks during certain stages of the embarkation before tonight is over, then nothing can prevent one of the most sanguinary and desperate fights in history.

Gallipoli and the Triumphant Retreat 169

The movement which at this moment is going on is the one which, from the day of landing, everyone here has most dreaded. I heard it said on the day of landing, and it has been commonplace ever since, that though the experiences of landing were bad enough one thing would be worse, and that was if it ever fell to our lot to have to get off again.

The only chance is to get the troops away without the enemy, of whom there are 85,000 at Anzac and Suvla, having a suspicion of it. The enemy cannot actually see the ground round the landing point, but there is an off-shoot from the main ridge to the north, from which he could look over our inner ridge, and into Ariburnu Point and half of the North Beach. It was known as 'Sniper's Nest' because he habitually sniped from there at night with a machine-gun. From Sniper's Nest he can just see the tip of one landing site, and all boats moving to or from them.

The plan at Anzac was quite different from that employed or is ever likely to be employed elsewhere. The whole normal garrison of every section of the firing line, divided into three parties, amounting possibly to a thousand or two, would be left holding the whole five miles of the outside line, faced by 40,000 Turks. Everything depended on them keeping up the appearance of a normal night. The extremes of the line, and especially those on the far left, were as much as three miles away, up steep, tortuous and empty gullies. Men would have to leave them at least one hour, and in some cases two hours, before they left the centre.

That last party was known as the Die Hards, they were not asked to volunteer. They were deliberately chosen, because the authorities wanted to get the men whom they themselves thought suitable. The result was quite extraordinary. Competition to stay behind in this batch was very keen, and in some units the commanding officers were flooded with complaints from men who had not been chosen, asking if there was anything against their record which had caused them to be overlooked.

...The uppermost thought in the mind of every man I have spoken to is regret at leaving the little mountain cemeteries, which every valley and hillside contains, for a week past, at any time of day, you saw small parties of men carefully lettering in the half-obliterated name of some comrade on a rough wooden cross, or carefully raking the mound, and bordering it neatly with fuse caps from fallen shells. The demand on ordnance for wood for crosses has been extraordinary. I noticed some chaplains sowing wattle and manuka on the graves. The men believe the Turks will respect these graveyards. Indeed many Australian soldiers have been writing letters to leave in their dugouts for 'Abdul', telling him what a clean fighter they think he has been, and wishing him au revoir.

The GOVERNOR-GENERAL's Surprise

Late in November 1975, Gough Whitlam asked the Men and Women of Australia to vote for him in the coming 13 December election and urged them to recall November 11. 'Remembrance Day 1975. Remember that day. Mr Fraser's day of shame.' And then he went on to further qualify it: 'a day that will live in infamy'.

Whitlam adapted the phrase from the famous opening to President Franklin D Roosevelt's address to his nation: 'Yesterday, December 7, 1941 – a date which will live in infamy – the United States of America was suddenly and deliberately attacked by naval and air forces of the Empire of Japan.'

The parallels were there. A few days earlier, on 11 November, Gough Whitlam had been sunk by an attack he had never expected: his dismissal as prime minister of Australia by the man he thought was 'on side', the man he appointed governor-general, Sir John Kerr.

'The dismissal of Whitlam, to shrewd observers,' Professor Geoffrey Blainey wrote in 2005, 'seemed to be one of the most momentous and far-reaching events in Australian history – an event like the start of World War I in 1914 or the acute Depression of the 1930s. Now, 30 years later, while the dismissal appears less momentous, it still stands as a major and nation-shaking event.'

This nation-shaking event, our greatest Constitutional crisis, was brought about by the egos of three very different men.

Urbane and autocratic, eloquent and witty, with a droll habit of addressing his colleagues as 'comrade', Prime Minister Gough Whitlam, 59, was adored by millions. They saw him as the Messiah who after 23 years had led them from the Opposition wilderness. His charisma was indisputable. But not even his ecstatic idolators would deny that Gough, as they called him, was a man of prodigious vanity.

Malcolm Fraser, 45, his political opponent, was stiff and aloof, utterly ruthless and with a boundless command of indignation. His face had all the emotion of the Easter Island monoliths it resembled. A Western District grazier, he showed no discernible charm or wit, but, like Whitlam, had an ego to match his towering height. Both men displayed the imperious confidence that comes with a wealthy family and a good school.

The man in between, Sir John Kerr, the silver-maned son of a boilermaker from working-class Balmain, had made his mark as a flamboyant lawyer. He had joined the ALP as a young man and was a union legal advisor before being elevated to Chief Justice of New South Wales. Although he was said to be a 'pre-war socialist' he enjoyed the good life, respected the Monarchy and relished the pomp and perks of his high office.

Kerr's upbringing was very different, but like Whitlam and Fraser, his vanity was considerable. When the prime minster injured it, using him as little more than a rubber stamp and taking the governor-general's consent for granted, he signed his political death warrant.

On the day Kerr issued the warrant, 11 November 1975, Australia was going through the most volatile and turbulent period in our modern political history.

Less than three years before, in December 1972, Gough Whitlam's Labor Party had been swept into office on a tsunami of excitement.

Whitlam, virtually single-handedly, had done it, and even many Liberal voters agreed that, as his campaign slogan had it, 'It's Time'. In an astonishing first few weeks in government Whitlam, once again virtually single-handedly, initiated radical reforms. Aborigines, foreign affairs, the arts, the environment, social welfare – the changes were so rapid, so dramatic and so wide ranging that most Australians felt a surge of patriotic pride that was fresh and new. Many felt their country was undergoing a Renaissance that reinvigorated a nation that for too long had been moribund, drifting under the torpor of lacklustre Liberal administrations. By the end of the following year, Whitlam could point with pride to 250 bills running to 2200 pages – three times as many pages as the Liberals in their last year in power. It was an exhilarating roller-coaster ride.

But there were those who wanted to get off the roller-coaster, slow it down or preferably stop it. The Coalition of the Liberal and National parties, which controlled the Senate, had blocked 20 per cent of these 250 bills – some of them election promises – and had tried to provoke a new election by blocking the government's supply bills. Without supply the government had no money to run the country.

Whitlam called the Coalition's bluff and agreed to the double dissolution elections – both Houses of Parliament were dissolved and a new election was called for May 1974. Labor was returned to government, although with a smaller majority. 'We were not defeated. We just didn't win enough seats to form a government,' said the Opposition Leader Billy Snedden, providing the nation with a welcome belly laugh and a laugh line that lives on to this day. But the truth was, the election was one of the closest in our history. It took 10 days for the results to become clear and when they did Labor and the Coalition each had secured 29 Senate seats. Two conservative Independents won the remaining Senate seats and when the Snedden laughter subsided, the threat to block supply was still on the Coalition's agenda. 'From May 1974,' Whitlam's speechwriter Graham Freudenberg wrote, 'the Labor Government was under siege. At no time thereafter could it plan confidently on more than six months of existence at a time. It lived in the expectation that each November and each May it would face another fight for Supply in the Senate.'

And now the Coalition had a new leader, the ambitious and aggressive Malcolm Fraser. If the government's actions were sufficiently 'extraordinary and reprehensible', and unless the prime minister called a double dissolution before June 1976, Malcolm Fraser promised that the Coalition, with its narrow majority in the Senate, would once again block supply. The opportunity came soon enough in a rolling series of 'Affairs'.

Gough Whitlam, a visionary, was never noted for his interest in economics. Others in the Cabinet were no better: his soon to be sacked treasurer, Frank Crean, likened the Cabinet's budget discussions to a debate in a lunatic asylum. Paul Keating, a minister in the last weeks of the government, said the Cabinet meetings 'were mayhem . . . much of it entirely undisciplined'. And the feeling that, economically, things were spinning out of control was exacerbated by the man who replaced Crean as treasurer, the Deputy Prime Minister Jim Cairns. Loved by some, loathed by others – there was no halfway – Jim Cairns, though he coyly denied it, was clearly smitten by Junie Morosi, his sultry principal private secretary, the first woman to hold such a position to a senior federal minister. Inevitably the romance became known as The Junie Morosi Affair. [See page 254.] Cairns was also making a series of grossly incompetent and bizarre errors involving memory loss, his son (and staffer) Phillip's business dealings – involving overseas Arab loans – and a signed authorisation giving a Melbourne businessman a 2.5 per cent 'brokerage fee' for loans he might raise for the Commonwealth of Australia. Cairns's blunders and his barely concealed love life eventually forced Whitlam to sack him for misleading Parliament.

A few days later Caucus removed him as deputy leader and installed dull but dependable Frank Crean.

Bill Hayden replaced Cairns as treasurer and began to rein in Labor's economic excesses. By now, however, more than a million people were living below the poverty line. Petrol prices were leaping; unemployment had trebled since 1972 to a quarter of a million; inflation, at 16.9 per cent, had quadrupled; and interest rates soared to 11.5 per cent. Budget expenditure was set to increase by 42 per cent, double the figure for 1973–74, which was itself the largest increase in two decades. In nine months since the 1974 election Whitlam's approval rating had plummeted from 57 per cent to 35 per cent and, worse, his disapproval rate doubled to more than 50 per cent. It was not the time for another double dissolution.

But that was what the Coalition was determined to have. All he needed, Fraser had said, was an 'extraordinary and reprehensible circumstance'.

The Juni Morosi Affair, the Loans Affair and its bizarre offshoot, the Khemlani Affair, gave him plenty of circumstances.

Rex Connor initiated the Loans Affair – an audacious attempt to raise a colossal $US4 billion, the biggest foreign loan ever authorised by the federal government and an amount that exceeded the combined foreign debt of all Australian governments. Connor was determined to 'buy back the farm', to give Australia ownership of its booming gas, oil and minerals industries. It would be a 'temporary loan' – a 20-year temporary loan.

In December 1974, while Sir John Kerr and his wife were at the ballet, a hasty night meeting of the executive council – Whitlam, Murphy, Cairns and Connor – authorised the raising of the $US4 billion. Foolishly, the governor-general agreed to sign the minutes of the meeting, at which he was not present and to which he had not been invited. Whitlam had used Kerr as a rubber stamp. Kerr resented this but kept his peace, and by staying silent reinforced Whitlam's confidence that he had the governor-general's support.

The public knew nothing of the proposed loan. Few Cabinet ministers knew. 'By even thinking of raising money to govern without the Senate's approval of supply,' Clive James wrote, 'Whitlam was preparing to govern without a parliament – the very thing the governor-general's powers are designed to stop.

'While proposing to govern without a parliament, Whitlam was already governing without a cabinet. Scarcely anyone knew about the Loans scheme being cooked up, its secrecy a tacit avowal of its fundamental unreality.' By the following month, the authority to raise the loan was withdrawn. By February, it was back on the agenda as a $US2 billion loan. By May, Whitlam believed the attempts to raise foreign loans had once again been abandoned. Too late, however, to prevent the unravelling of the Loans Affair.

In May 1975, helped by drip feeds from an alarmed Treasury, the media was beginning to publish details of a covert and extremely unorthodox attempt by the Government to raise 'petrodollars' from Middle East oil sheikhs. The broker, Tirath Khemlani, a fly-by-night Pakistan commodity dealer living in London, was named in Parliament. Khemlani was later jailed in the US, for trying to pass stolen travellers cheques.

But on 2 September, Whitlam told Parliament that the Minerals and Energy Minister Rex Connor had assured him that there had been no further negotiations with Khemlani after 20 May – a claim Connor repeated on 9 October, the day after the Melbourne *Herald* carried fresh and dramatic news of what was now called the Khemlani Affair. The paper claimed that Connor wanted to raise up to $US8 billion in two parts at 8.22 per cent interest over two years. The terms of the loan meant that Australia would have to pay back $US39 billion – around $US250 billion in today's terms.

Nicknamed 'the Strangler', Connor was a taciturn politician feared on both sides of the House. He denied the report and said he would sue the *Herald*.

A *Herald* reporter, Peter Game, who had chased Khemlani

around the world, met him again in Melbourne. Khemlani brought with him telexes that contradicted Connor's claims. They showed that Connor had continued to ask Khemlani to negotiate loans after Whitlam had assured Parliament that Connor had told him he had stopped. Just five days after the *Herald* broke the news, Connor was sacked for causing Whitlam to mislead Parliament. He was replaced by the young up-and-comer Paul Keating.

The next day, Malcolm Fraser announced that, because of the extraordinary and reprehensible circumstance, he would defer finance for the government. 'The Opposition now has no choice,' he said in his sanctimonious monotone. 'The Labor Government 1972–75 has been the most incompetent and disastrous government in the history of Australia.' His party would block the budget in the Senate until Whitlam called an election.

Whitlam responded predictably in his own, booming, even more distinctive tones; his government had survived the same tactic in 1974. 'We will not yield to blackmail. We will not be panicked.' It was coming down to a battle of egos, a question of which man would break first.

For three weeks the constitutional crisis heightened as the parties confronted each other in Parliament and around the country. Whitlam was confident that the Senate was on the point of passing the supply bills, that the Liberals would lose their nerve. If Whitlam was wrong, government money for payment to public servants and government contractors would run out by 30 November. The crisis could then end in one of only two ways. He would buckle and call an election or the governor-general would sack him. Whitlam, however, was confident that he wouldn't be sacked.

Two men begged to differ. Bill Hayden, the new treasurer, met Sir John to brief him on alternative financial arrangements. Hayden was disturbed to find that the governor-general was more interested in discussing Whitlam's fighting abilities. 'How do you think you'd go if there was an election?' he asked Hayden. Hayden told him, 'We'd be done like a dinner,' but Kerr thought that Whitlam was a fighter, and could come back. Hayden, alarmed, left Yarralumla and ordered his driver to take him not to the airport, but direct to Whitlam's office. A former policeman, his 'copper's instinct' told him that Kerr was going to sack Whitlam. He found Whitlam entirely at ease. 'He was standing against the wall even larger than life. He was fiddling his spectacles around in his hand. He said to me, "No comrade, he wouldn't have the guts for that."'

As a young lawyer, Bob Ellicott QC, a junior minister in the Opposition, once had an office on the same floor of the same chambers as Whitlam's and Kerr's, and the three knew each other well. Ellicott had risen to become Commonwealth solicitor-general, and, as it transpired, knew Kerr better than Whitlam. Ellicott believed that Kerr might use the reserve power that the Queen's representative in Australia had to act on his own behalf. In a media release Ellicott warned that, 'The Prime Minister is treating the Governor-General as a mere automaton with no public will of his own, sitting at Yarralumla waiting to do his bidding. Nothing could be further from the truth . . .

'The Governor-General has at least two clear constitutional prerogatives he can exercise: the right to dismiss his ministers and appoint others and the right to refuse a dissolution of the parliament or of either house.'

Whitlam said that Kerr phoned him to say, 'This Ellicott thing, it's all bullshit isn't it?' and Whitlam asked his attorney-general and solicitor-general to prepare a 6000-word opinion confirming that blunt assessment. He was confident that Kerr was 'on-side'. When colleagues asked him about the governor-general's position, Whitlam would reassure them: 'Kerr will do the right thing comrade. I'm as confident of this as I am about anything in my career.'

Kerr, meanwhile, privately consulted Sir Garfield Barwick, the chief justice of the High Court, who concurred with Ellicott. The governor-general had the power to sack Whitlam and instruct the incoming prime minister to promptly call a new federal election.

The debate over the legality and ethics of blocking supply to force an election was not new. In Opposition, Whitlam and Lionel Murphy, later to join the High Court bench, had affirmed the legality of such tactics and had tried them no fewer than 170 times while out of office. The Liberals, when in office, strongly disagreed on the question of their legality and fair play. Now the two parties were performing backflips on the question. Now it was the Liberals threatening to block supply and Labor taking the high ground.

Less than four weeks later, at 12. 40 pm, on 11 November 1975, Whitlam went to Government House to formally request that Kerr approve a half-Senate election. He had rejected Malcolm Fraser's compromise of an election for both houses in May 1976 and instead pinned his hopes on an immediate half-Senate election that he hoped would give him power in the upper house.

In the governor-general's Yarralumla study, as he reached into his inside pocket to pass over the formal advice, Whitlam found that Kerr, instead, was passing him a letter. It outlined his reasons for refusing the half-Senate election and notified Whitlam that he was dismissing him and his government.

Kerr had been suspicious of Whitlam and possibly planning this moment ever since Whitlam had made a flippant remark less than three weeks before. At Government House he had said to Kerr that it might be 'a question of whether I get to the Queen first for your recall, or you get in first with my dismissal'. Laughter all around – but Kerr was not amused. 'Quite devastated,' he said later. Now, metaphorically, the governor-general had beaten the prime minister to the phone.

'He had his warning,' Kerr said later. 'The ball was in his court.' Kerr said that in the fraction of time between his telling Whitlam of his intention to dismiss him and his passing over of the letter

Whitlam had one lifeline, to 'negotiate to go to the people as Prime Minister . . . had he done so I would have agreed.'

'Things then happened as I had foreseen,' Kerr said in his autobiography, *Matters of Judgement*. 'Mr Whitlam jumped up, looked urgently around the room, looked at the telephones and said sharply, "I must get in touch with the Palace at once."' It was too late for that, Kerr told him. 'He said, "Why?" and I told him, "Because you are no longer Prime Minister. These documents tell you so and why."'

Whitlam heard Kerr say, 'We shall all have to live with this.' The former prime minister had the presence of mind to reply, 'You certainly will,' and the good grace to shake hands with Kerr as the governor-general wished him farewell and good luck in the coming election. It was their last conversation. At 1.30 pm, Malcolm Fraser, waiting in another room, was sworn in as a caretaker prime minister on the condition that he immediately call an election.

Whitlam, meanwhile, went back to the Lodge and sat down to a late lunch, a steak. Why he chose to have a substantial lunch without notifying any of his Cabinet is perplexing. Whitlam finally summoned a small circle of colleagues, the deputy prime minister, the leader of the House, the attorney-general, the head of the prime minister's department and his scriptwriter, and told them the news. 'We all sat there like stunned mullets,' said Fred Daly, the leader of the House of Representatives. None thought to notify Labor's leader in the Senate, Ken Wriedt, that he was now the Opposition leader in the upper house, and not two hours after Whitlam had left Parliament to get the governor-general's rubber stamp on a half-Senate election Labor Senators, ignorant of the fact that they were out of government, passed the Budget, imagining that Fraser had finally caved in.

At 3 o'clock Whitlam returned to Parliament and on his way met young Paul Keating, three weeks a minister. 'You're sacked!' he said as he brushed on by, leaving a bewildered Keating plaintively calling after him, 'What for?' In Parliament, Whitlam moved a motion that the House express no confidence in the caretaker prime minister and it was approved. The Speaker was instructed to see the governor-general and ask him to commission Mr Whitlam again but was told Sir John Kerr was unavailable until 4.45.

At that time, Whitlam, his eyes glowing with self-righteous indignation and staring fiercely into the middle distance, was standing on the steps of Parliament House behind the governor-general's secretary, David Smith. There was the hint of a grim smile on his lips as Smith read the proclamation dissolving Parliament. Smith concluded, 'God save the Queen', and Whitlam stepped to the microphone: 'Ladies and gentlemen, well may we say "God save the Queen", because nothing will save the Governor-General. The proclamation you have just heard read by the Governor-General's official secretary was countersigned "Malcolm Fraser", who will undoubtedly go down in history as Kerr's cur.'

As the crowd roared and cheered, he ended with this rousing command: 'Maintain your rage and enthusiasm throughout the campaign for the election now to be held and until polling day.'

Around Australia the news stunned everyone. There was agitation for a national strike – Bob Hawke, the unions' leader, defused it. In the pubs of Balmain and Carlton, hotheads leapt on bars and called for the barricades to go up. There were no takers, though there were demonstrations around the country; Fraser was egg-bombed; and real mail bombs were posted eight days later, one of them injuring two staffers of the Queensland premier. But though the country was fiercely divided and the respect for the position of the governor-general almost irrevocably damaged, the army was not called out. Gough Whitlam had too much respect for the Constitution, and the country went peacefully enough to the polls.

On 13 December 1975, the Coalition won the election in a landslide. In 1977 Labor's vote plummeted even further and Whitlam retired, a Labor martyr. Sir John Kerr died a lonely and tragic man. Fraser governed until 1984 when, beaten by Labor's new Messiah, Bob Hawke, he made a tearful apology to the Liberal Party.

Thirty years on Whitlam is still revered and – astonishingly – reconciled with his tormentor, Fraser, who by now had turned his energies to ceaseless attacks on . . . the Liberal Party.

SHANE WARNE.
Now You See It, Now You Don't

I looked up and saw this chubby cheeky bloke with blond spiked hair. 'What do you want me to do?' he asked.

'Just bowl me a leg break.'

Without any real warm-up he bowled this leg break which curved half a metre and spun just as far! It was seemingly effortless, yet a magnificent delivery.

'&%#@ me,' I said to myself. 'What have we got here?'

– *TJ Over the Top*, Terry Jenner (Australian test spin bowler of the 1970s), with Ken Piesse

What we have here – it goes without saying – is Shane Warne, one of *Wisden*'s five cricketers of the 20th century, perhaps the greatest bowler cricket has known and certainly the supreme spin bowler. The man who has taken more Test wickets and turned the course of more Test matches than any other. The man who has made more headlines than Bradman, Lillee and the entire current Australian XI and the 12th man put together. Too many headlines, alas, along the lines of the *London Daily Mirror*'s: 'Shame Warne. Married cricket legend harasses a mum for sex with obscene phone calls.'

From 20 metres Shane Warne can hit a 50 cent piece at 100 kilometres an hour but off the pitch he can't seem to stay on the straight and narrow. One of the boys, he seems recklessly determined not to grow up. It is an attitude that has cost him dearly.

'At the end of the day, it's cost me probably. . . a chance to captain Australia,' he told Jana Wendt in the *Bulletin*. '. . .my marriage is breaking down, we're getting a divorce. It's cost me all that and it's cost me a sponsorship. It's cost me lots of stuff. But I don't sit here and think every day about "why did I do this?" I don't think like that. . . It's done and the more you harp on it, the more you whinge about it. . . the more it stiffs with your head, the more it plays on your mind and the more it affects your general life, everyday life. . . It affects absolutely everything. . . What can I do about it? Sit here and cry and whinge?'

The tragedy is, Shane Warne brings so much happiness to so many Australian men. (Women rarely admit to liking Warney.) On the field he is sublime, the magician who rediscovered the black art of leg spin bowling, thought, until he came along, to have gone the way of the dodo. Watching Warne bowl is bliss. Simplicity itself. He grips the ball, turns, takes a few steps and rips it down, fizzing, curving, jumping or shooting low, staying straight or breaking almost at right angles: with Warne you never know. And, time and again, his baffling ball – take your pick from the zooter, the flipper, the drifter, the topspinner, the wrong 'un – takes wickets at the psychological moment: unexpected, just when the game seems to be getting away from Australia, or so anticipated that you would put money on it.

And best of all, he saves his best for the big stage.

Warne's most famous ball, the Ball of the Century, the Wonder Ball, That Ball, as it has become variously known, typically came at the perfect psychological moment: the very first ball he bowled in a Test against England. Paul Barry in *Spun Out: The Shane Warne Story*, describes it:

The bare facts of it are that at 3.06 p.m., on 4 June 1993, a leg break from Warne landed outside [Mike] Gatting's leg stump at Old Trafford and spun 60 centimetres or roughly two feet to the left, clipping the top of the stumps and removing the bail. But that doesn't begin to describe how amazing it was. I remember thinking it was impossible for the ball to have spun past Gatting's bat and hit the wicket. And that's clearly what Gatting thought too. Looking back at the tapes, what immediately strikes you is how quickly the ball comes through and how slowly the batsman departs.

Gatting departed slowly because he was completely discombobulated. England's stout skipper stayed in his crease, looking at the umpire, for a good 10 seconds. He simply couldn't believe that the ball had got past him and hit his wicket. Some commentators felt the same way: 'How anyone can spin a ball the width of Gatting boggles the mind,' English sports writer Martin Johnson observed. Graham Gooch, an English captain of the same era, pointed out, 'If it had been a cheese roll it would never have got past him.' That was much later, of course. For a long time, the Ball from Hell was no laughing matter to the English. In effect, they lost their Ashes bid in those few astonishing seconds.

Warne was 23, an overweight boy from Black Rock, when he bowled Gatting and after it his life could never be the same. 'That ball sort of changed my whole life,' he told Jana Wendt. 'Suddenly people wanted to know who I hung out with, where I hung out. . . what I was actually doing. . . I'm not trying to say, "Oh, poor Shane-o" but it was bloody difficult getting followed around all the time. . . leave your hotel room and there'd be four photographers following you and jumping in a car and you'd go down the pub or you'd do whatever and they'd be waiting out the front. That was hard.'

The index to Paul Barry's book tells the sorry story: AIS Cricket

Academy, departure from; unwillingness to train; Australian Test team, sacking from; betting scandal; drug scandal; gambling, betting on cricket; Indian Central Bureau of Investigation; rock star treatment; schoolboy's photo incident; sex scandals; sledging; smoking; suspension; women; world Anti-Doping Agency. None of it amounts to much, and most of it borders on farce. Still, with a little commonsense and a lot of character, Shane Warne could have been, like Keith Miller, a rebel revered as a brilliant cricketer and a fine man.

The joke goes that a poll of 600 women was asked if they'd sleep with Shane Warne. Seventy-two per cent of respondents said: Never again!

If only Shane had said the same.

LEN LAWSON.
A Monster Behind the Mask

For most of us the first – and with luck – the worst deception we encounter is Santa Claus. Or rather, we don't encounter Santa Claus. Instead we discover that the jolly old man with the flowing white beard doesn't exist; he is no more than the centrepiece of a gigantic conspiracy to hoodwink, with the best of intentions though it may be.

Learning the truth about Santa Claus can be devastating, but it's a realisation that has usually dawned slowly and we learn to live with it, to become part of the conspiracy ourselves.

For a generation of Australian boys, however, the Lone Avenger deception was bewildering and disillusioning. It took years before we got over it.

The Lone Ranger was a hero to those boys born in the 1940s, a decade before television came to Australia. Until then Australian kids had to subsist on an entertainment diet of playing on the streets, jumping from the chook-house roof, listening to radio serials and reading – comics preferably.

We loved comics. Boys loved no comic more than *The Phantom,* the ghost who walks, the man who cannot die. Lee Falk, we all knew, created the Phantom and Mandrake the Magician, both masterpieces of the art that had begun in America, and was therefore peerless. Australian adventure comics simply couldn't compete.

There was one exception: the Lone Avenger. Possibly related to the more famous Lone Ranger, the Lone Avenger was immensely popular, at his peak selling 73,000 comics an issue.

The Lone Avenger began as a vigilante and then settled down to be the Sheriff of Redrock. He wore trim-fitting white trousers teamed with a grass-green shirt and brown boots, topping this striking ensemble with a red hood, through the eye slits of which no pupils were visible. The hood had no opening for the Lone Avenger's mouth, which must have made eating cumbersome. Above the hood he wore a handsome, white, 10-gallon hat. The Lone Avenger's sidekick was Deputy Sheriff Bull Malone, who was not overly bright and whose cauliflower ears betrayed a violent past, possibly as a forward for St George. The Lone Avenger rode Midnight, a dark blue horse who seemed to be perpetually in motion, either galloping over landscapes littered with skulls, or rearing majestically at the slightest invitation, often on a picturesque mesa.

The Lone Avenger's name was Paul Nicolls. Pretty girls in tight blouses, dance hall girls and young ladies from the east, often crossed his path. And he had a girlfriend, Caroline Grey, the town schoolmarm. One day walking down a country lane with him, Caroline says: 'Paul dear you can take that mask off now. Nobody's going to see you out here!' He says: 'Sure, Caroline. Funny thing, I'm so used to it.'

Len Lawson created the Lone Avenger at 19. By 25, with the comic selling 73,000 copies an issue, he was the highest-paid black-and-white artist in Australia. We Lone Avenger fans were proud of Len Lawson. Here was that rare thing, an Australian comic strip artist as good – almost – as the fabled Lee Falk.

Then we discovered that like the Lone Avenger, Len Lawson's

real character was hooded. Far from being the greatest artist Australia had ever produced we found that he was … well, we kids weren't quite sure. All we could glean from the newspaper stories in May 1954 was that he was going to hang. Suddenly those of us old enough to follow the court reports shed our comic book illusions. This was real, adult life. And Lennie Lawson, we found, was far from the man we imagined him to be, the alter ego of our hero the Lone Avenger.

A classic nerd with a very nasty twist, Lawson had driven five models, aged from 15 to 22, to bushland near Sydney's northern beaches. They believed they were going on a photo shoot. Instead Lawson bound and gagged them at gunpoint, raped two and indecently assaulted the others. He was quickly captured and sentenced to death but soon after, when the death penalty was abolished, began a life sentence.

He was released in 1961. Five months later, in October, he met Jane Bower, aged 16. Her boss described her as 'the prettiest girl, kind and sweet'. Over the next month, Lawson ingratiated himself with her parents until they were happy to allow her to go to his flat to have her portrait painted. He bludgeoned her unconscious with a sock full of sand, tied her up and raped and stabbed her. He put her on his bed and wrote across her stomach, 'God forgive me, Len.'

The next morning he stormed into the chapel of the exclusive Sydney Church of England Girls Grammar School in the southern highlands of New South Wales. The last time Lawson had been there he'd come unannounced and introducing himself as an author researching a novel set in a girls' school. He'd been welcomed, joined the staff for lunch and presented the headmistress, Jean Turnbull, with one of his works, a painting of Christ.

This time he came with a loaded Remington and rope in a bag. Jean Turnbull – ironically she was called Bull by the girls, an echo of the Lone Avenger's sidekick – demanded to know what he was doing. Lawson, ranting, told her that he had already killed a girl and he was prepared to kill again. He would hold the students hostage until he could exchange them for Tania Verstak, then Miss Australia; Marlene Matthews, an attractive Olympic sprinter; and a nun he knew. They would ensure his safe passage out of the country. In the middle of his ravings Lawson looked out the window and saw police running to the chapel.

'I'll shoot you all now,' he screamed as Jean Turnbull grappled with him. She took a bullet in her hand. Wendy Luscombe, 15, was shot in the heart.

Once again he began a life sentence. Twelve years later, in Parramatta jail he charmed Sharon Hamilton, a visiting entertainer, a go-go dancer. Without warning Lawson put a shiv. to her neck and, in a cliché straight from the action comic screamed: 'Don't anyone move or I'll let her have it!' A fellow inmate punched Lawson to the ground and he was held down.

After spending a total of 48 years in jail, Len Lawson, 76, died in his cell in 2003.

THE RIPPED OFF

Exploitation, esp.
of those who cannot
prevent or counter it

RUPERT MURDOCH and the Man He Saved

Rupert Keith Murdoch and Rupert Max Stuart were in Adelaide, and in trouble, for related reasons. Rupert Murdoch, 27, the owner of the Adelaide *News* was charged with seditious libel – treason. Rupert Max Stuart, a year younger, was waiting to be hanged.

Murdoch was the son of a famous newspaperman, Keith Murdoch. Keith Murdoch had tried and failed to break into Fleet Street but in 1915, at the age of 30, his life changed dramatically when he spent a short time – perhaps as little as four days – on the battlefields of Gallipoli. He was described at that time by an English journalist with him as 'a man of forceful personality, combining keen love of power with an intense devotion to his country'.

Keith Murdoch was shocked at what he saw at Gallipoli. He wrote a letter to the Australian Prime Minister which he copied for the British Prime Minister. The letter, a savage attack on the handling of the Gallipoli, or Dardanelles Campaign, influenced the decision to pull out and made Murdoch's journalistic name. Les Carlyon, in his authoritative book *Gallipoli,* says the letter 'is a farrago of fact and gossip, sense and nonsense, sometimes fluttery and sometimes tough, pro-Australian and anti-British . . .' But as Murdoch's son Rupert said seven decades on: 'Oh sure, it may not have been fair but it changed history, that letter.'

Keith Murdoch came home a celebrity and in time became Sir Keith Murdoch, newspaper publisher. When he died, 21-year-old Rupert inherited the Adelaide *News*, the dreary second newspaper in a sleepy town, the first of many newspapers and many towns that Murdoch was to shake awake.

The lives of the two Ruperts came together in 1958 when Stuart, an illiterate itinerant Aborigine who drank and spoke in pidgin English, was found guilty of raping and murdering a nine-year-old girl, Mary Hattam, in a cave three kilometres from Ceduna. The time of the murder was put at between 2 pm and 8.30 pm on Saturday 20 December.

Max Stuart's father, Paddy, was a stockman and at the age of 11 Stuart left home to work on stations around Alice Springs. Still a teenager, he fought bare-knuckled in Jimmy Sharman's sideshow boxing tents and learned to drink heavily. Mary Hattam and her two brothers had been playing on the beach when, at 2.30 pm, the boys went to get a tub to use as a boat, leaving Mary alone. At 4 pm, Mary's father went to the beach. Mary was nowhere to be seen. Her body was found in a small cave eight hours later. She had been raped and mutilated.

The next morning, police brought in a two Aboriginal 'trackers' who found footprints leading to the Funland carnival, but the fun fair was gone. Funland had left Ceduna the day after the murder and headed for Whyalla. Many Aborigines had visited the carnival at Ceduna and several suspects were brought to the beach but the trackers said their footprints didn't match those at the cave.

Max Stuart, meanwhile, had been arrested drunk at 9.30 on the Saturday night and was in custody. Following his release on Sunday morning, he was picked up again by police on the Monday, working nearby for the Australian Wheat Board. The police made him walk barefoot across sand and the trackers agreed that his footprints matched those of the killer.

Stuart signed a typed confession with the only English word he knew, misspelling his name in block letters: ROPERT.

Convicted and sentenced to hang, Stuart had prepared a statement from the dock. Because he could not read it, he asked that a court official do so. The judge refused and Stuart made this verbal statement: 'I cannot read or write. Never been to school. I did not see the little girl. Police hit me, choke me. Make me said these words. They say I kill her.'

At the core of the case against Stuart was his confession, allegedly dictated in the company of six policemen. 'It was a piece of quite good English,' Tom Farrell, a *Sydney Morning Herald* journalist said. 'All the verbs and nouns in the right place and not the sort of language that an Aborigine would use anywhere.' In 1958 that was a reasonable comment. And Father Thomas Dixon, a Catholic priest who had seen Stuart on 10 May – less than two weeks before he was to be hanged – agreed. Father Dixon spoke Stuart's Arrernte language, and had no doubt that Stuart could not possibly have dictated the articulate statement.

Anthropologist Ted Strehlow, who also spoke Arrernte, agreed that the confession could not be genuine and his sworn affidavit led to an appeal to the High Court. That failed, as did another appeal to the Privy Council. But the appeals meant that Stuart's execution date was pushed back.

In the meantime, Murdoch and his editor Rohan Rivett had begun a fierce campaign questioning the confession. They sent Father Dixon to Queensland with a *News* reporter to find Funland. The two caught up with the fun fair at Atherton on 27 July.

'I wouldn't know anything about his [Stuart's] movements,' Norman Gieseman, the proprietor of Funland, told them. 'We only saw him from two till four. That's when he was at the fun fair.'

Gieseman was adamant. 'I will stand up to that but nothing else.' (He had sacked Stuart on the day of the murder for getting drunk with a 15-year-old boy from Funland.) Nevertheless Gieseman had nominated, almost precisely, the time span when the little girl was abducted. Two women confirmed Gieseman's recollection, one of them Mrs Gieseman, and the other Betty Hopes, who had been in the skittles stall in the same tent as Stuart. 'Max did not leave the stall all the time and he was in full view of me.'

The government of the day, led by Sir Thomas Playford, was determined that Stuart would hang, the eighth man to go to the gallows under his regime. This new evidence, however, and the aggressive and relentless campaign of the *News*, demanded a Royal Commission. It was a farce. The *News* splashed the headline, written by Murdoch, 'THESE COMMISSIONERS CANNOT DO THE JOB'.

Adelaide, a staid country town run by the Establishment, was in turmoil. But around the nation the *News* campaign had begun to bite. Furious, Playford hit back with a string of charges against Rivett and Murdoch, one of them seditious libel.

Stuart was saved from the gallows, but sentenced to life in prison. Then in 1973, two cadet journalist on the Melbourne *Herald,* Jenni Brown and Pamela Graham, disclosed that the chairman of the Parole Board, Sir Roderic Chamberlain, had made it clear to them that Stuart would never be released and that he said, 'I would have pulled the lever myself.'

Stuart was paroled in 1974.

Rupert Murdoch today heads an empire unimaginable in 1959. Newspapers, magazines, film, television, cable, the internet, sports teams, books, satellite broadcasting, his News Corp interests and influence has played a role in shaping Australia and much of the world.

Now an American citizen, a decision made purely for commercial reasons, Murdoch is nonetheless an archetypical Australian. It's in his accent and in his actions. Blunt, pragmatic, in awe of no-one, he marries his boundless ambition with decisiveness and vision. He understands the possibilities. He showed that first in the Adelaide *News* campaign.

How does he remember those years?

In 2002, Murdoch told the *7.30 Report,* 'I remember being tried for treason. We were very proud of the *News* for the constant [steady] circulation. It was not a popular cause to take up, the case of an Aboriginal who, we felt, without making any judgment on whether he was guilty or not, we said that he had not had a fair trial. And we forced a change in that.'

Stuart, for his part, remembered Murdoch watching him in court. 'He wanted the truth you know.'

By then, Max Stuart had been Chairman of the Central Land Council and was among the official party that met the Queen in Alice Springs two years before.

He thanked Rupert Murdoch for saving his life. 'He done a good one, in my case,' he told the *7.30 Report*. 'I think he done a good thing. Otherwise, if we hadn't had Rupert Murdoch, I would have been down in Adelaide jail now, been buried there in unmarked grave.

'But thank Christ he came in.'

NED KELLY's Case. Still Not Closed

Had Ned Kelly's mother been sentenced to spend six weeks at the seaside, her son might have been a footnote in the short and violent history of bushranging: 'Edward (Ned) Kelly. Horse thief. Apprentice, 1870–1871 to Harry Power (see Power, Harry, last of the noted bushrangers)'.

Mrs Ellen Kelly, battling to bring up her family in appalling poverty, certainly could have done with a holiday. But it was her, and the Kelly family's, ill fortune to come up against a man with an implacable hatred of the Catholic Irish. Here was a hanging judge with a fear that unless the bog Irish Catholics were kept in check they could rise up as they had back in Ireland when he lived there and overthrow the established order. Sir Redmond Barry was the Protestant Irish son of a British general, the senior judge in the colony named after the ruling British monarch. Barry knew the Kellys: he had sentenced Ned's uncle to be hanged for arson.

Now Barry was sitting in judgment on what the Crown said was the attempted murder of a policeman but what was, in fact, little more than a farce. A fracas in a tiny crowded kitchen that was almost comical, the sort of slapstick scene that 30 years later had silent movie audiences in stitches. A villainous, lecherous landlord enters, gleefully twirling a wicked moustache. His eyes light up as a fair maiden comes within his grope. The heroine's sweetheart/brother/mother, outraged, come to her rescue, and the rounds of the kitchen ensue, with the villain, beaned by a frying pan as the piano accompanist supplies the sound effects, executing a slow, stiff-as-a plank pratfall.

Tragically, the rounds of the kitchen at the Kellys led to the jailing of Ned's mother and drove Ned and his brother to become fugitives. That, in turn, led to the shootout at Stringybark Creek and that led to the bank hold-ups, the creation of the very first superhero outfits and the Last Stand at Glenrowan. And that, finally, led to the legend of Ned Kelly.

It all happened for Ned Kelly in 26 mostly tumultuous years. But, long after his execution at Melbourne Gaol in 1880, he continues to fascinate. For some, he is simply a blowhard full of the worst aspects of his Irish blood, a thug who became a killer who intended to kill scores more. There is truth in that. But, there was another side to Kelly. And it is the combination of that side; his charisma, with its Irish charm, foibles and blarney; his chivalry and his bravery; and the fact that he was, as he claimed, 'a widow's son wronged' that has kept the legend of Ned Kelly alive. That and the helmet, of course.

But it all was triggered by the rounds of the kitchen and the shoot-out that followed at Stringybark Creek.

At Jerilderie, a town he held captive for two days, Ned handed over his 8300-word manifesto, an autobiographical document addressed to the Premier of the State, giving his side of the story. It told of the affray in the kitchen of his home and of the Stringybark killings and why Ned was adamant that he shot in self-protection. And it railed against the persecution he and his family had always suffered from 'the cowardly conduct of a parcel of big ugly fat-necked wombat headed big bellied magpie legged narrow hipped splay-footed sons of Irish bailiffs and English landlords which is better known as officers of the Victorian Police'.

At Jerilderie, we see the side of Ned that has inspired a Booker Prize novel, one of scores of fiction and non-fiction books, a $40 million Hollywood movie, numerous other television dramas and movies, including the first feature film ever made, and Sidney Nolan's famous sequence of 27 Ned Kelly paintings. At Jerilderie, Kelly was a charmer – men and women agreed – a fine figure of a man, with, the schoolteacher recalled, 'a lot of Don Quixote . . . a dreamer in his own way'.

Standing at the bar of the pub, Ned put his revolver down beside his glass. 'There's my revolver,' he told the assembly. 'Anyone here may take it and shoot me dead, but if I'm shot Jerilderie shall swim in its own blood.' Ned Kelly was not a heavy drinker, but he sometimes talked like one. He was foolhardy and, sometimes, foolish. 'I am a widow's son outlawed' is a memorable statement, but Ned continues, 'and my orders must be obeyed!' and the noble note of defiance becomes shrill and absurd.

Ned Kelly is an enigma. A braggart and a cool-headed killer. A brave man who came back to save his mates when he could have saved his own skin. (Had he been born 35 years later, Dame Mabel Brookes wrote in her autobiography, Ned might have won a Victoria Cross at Gallipoli.) An articulate and intelligent man who might have saved his life had he chosen to speak in his defence at his trial. A man who took his last walk, to the gallows, and talked about the flowers on the way. A man who wanted to start a revolution that would establish a Republic in north-east Victoria, but who had nothing to say at the last but a mumbled, 'I suppose it had to come to this.'

The Melbourne Gaol's Protestant Minister, John Cowley Coles, visited Ned, at Ned's request, shortly before his execution. Coles wrote:

> The man by no means looked a ruffian. He had a rather pleasant expression of countenance. He was one of the most powerfully

built and finest men that I ever saw. He treated me with great respect, listened to all I had to say, and knelt down by my side when I prayed . . . He answered me, 'I have heard all you said this morning referring to the address [a sermon Coles preached within Kelly's hearing, the text being Prepare to meet your God]. I believe it all. Although I have been bushranging I have always believed that when I die I have a God to meet.' He added, 'When I was in the bank at Jerilderie, taking the money, the thought came into my mind, if I am shot down at this moment, how can I meet my God?' I knelt down in the cell and prayed with him, he kneeling by my side.'

The foremost authority on Kelly, Ian Jones, best sums it up in *Ned Kelly: A Short Life*.

Because Ned Kelly was what he was, and did what he did, Australians will always speak and write about him in terms of their own gods or their own demons. This is the Kelly phenomenon today as in 1880. This is perhaps Ned Kelly's tragedy, yet it is also his triumph and the seed of his immortality.

Ned Kelly's parents, John 'Red' Kelly and Ellen Quinn, were married in the little church of St Francis, still standing in the heart of Melbourne, on Monday, 18 November 1850. Red had been a convict, ostensibly transported from Ireland for stealing two pigs. The reality may have been much darker. There are good reasons to believe that Red was an informer who caused two of his mates to be apprehended for cow stealing – one of them had been shot dead trying to escape.

Their first-born child, a girl, survived only briefly. Ellen then had a daughter, Anne. Then in December 1854, at Beveridge, 40 kilometres north of Melbourne on the road to Sydney, Edward 'Ned'

Kelly was born. Ellen would bear nine more children. Ned grew up a conscientious scholar who came second in his class and excelled at all games. He was a natural leader, his classmates remembered, and a brave boy. In 1862, aged 11, Ned heroically rescued a small boy from drowning, and in gratitude, the parents presented young Ned with a splendid green silk sash with a commemorative inscription. Ned was wearing that sash beneath his armour when made his Last Stand at Glenrowan.

A year after Ned's brave act of rescue, Red Kelly died and 12-year-old Ned became the man of the house, looking after his mother and six siblings. In 1867, the family moved to an 88-acre property on the Eleven Mile Creek near Greta in Victoria's north-east, where Ellen's family and her in-laws, small selector farmers, were frequently before the courts on charges of stock theft.

The north-east of Victoria was a bitterly divided community: squatters against selectors. The squatters, a small group of men who controlled the land from the founding days considered themselves the rightful owners and fought against any proposal to allow others to settle. From 1860, however, any man or single woman could select up to 320 acres and pay it off over time, provided that they lived on the land and cultivated it. Neither side was satisfied with the arrangement. The selectors, with reason, were bitter at the way the squatters, once they realised land reform was inevitable, had secured the best lands on their runs and entrenched themselves in positions of power. The police inevitably favoured the squatters.

At Greta, Ellen was among her family, the Quinn clan, and her in-laws, the Lloyds. Here, Ned first got into trouble with the law. In 1869, at 14, he was charged with assaulting a Chinese man, but the charge was dismissed. And, at Greta, the last of the notable bushrangers, Harry Power, recruited young Ned as his apprentice. A year after the assault charge, Ned was up before the magistrate at Benalla charged with being an accomplice of Power, but again the charge was dismissed. Then he was jailed for six months for throwing a hawker into a creek. Up to this point, Ned could be seen as a larrikin, something of a bully, but the sort of likely lad that can still be found in country towns. At heart they are decent enough and almost invariably go on to distinguish themselves in the town football and cricket teams before marrying and disappearing into the mists of domesticity.

In 1871, however, Ned, now a strapping youth, was found with a stolen horse and, when he resisted arrest, was brutally pistol-whipped. Ned claimed, and it was certainly true, that he hadn't realised the horse was stolen (he'd borrowed it from a friend), but he was sentenced to three years' hard labour at Beechworth, Pentridge and the *Sacramento*, a convict hulk moored at Williamstown. He came out at 19, probably intending to stay out of trouble, and spent three years working in a variety of jobs, but then he went back to horse stealing on a large and sophisticated scale.

The pivotal moment in the story of Ned Kelly arrived one April afternoon in 1878 when Constable Alex Fitzpatrick came to Greta to arrest Ned's 16-year-old brother Dan. Fitzpatrick had no authority to do so and was going against orders that stipulated that police officers were never to go alone to the Kellys. He was also going there after stopping, he admitted later, for 'some brandy and lemonade' at a pub on the way.

What happened next will never be known. Fitzpatrick, the Kellys claimed, made a pass at 15-year-old Kate Kelly and a brawl broke out. Mrs Kelly whacked Fitzpatrick with a shovel and, Fitzpatrick claimed, Ned appeared and shot him in the wrist. Ned claimed that he was many miles away at the time, but in any case the wound was so slight that a doctor testified that it 'might' have been caused by a bullet grazing the skin. The likelihood is that Ned was there and that Fitzpatrick, as he said, was grazed by a bullet from Ned's gun in a scuffle. But, whatever the truth – and Fitzpatrick was later dismissed from the police force because 'he could not be trusted out of sight' – the trouble in the kitchen was footling. Mrs Kelly bandaged the graze and Fitzpatrick rode off, seemingly at peace with the clan; instead, Mrs Kelly found herself charged with attempted murder. Fitzpatrick claimed he had been attacked by Ellen, Ned, Dan Kelly, their associate Bricky Williamson and Ned's brother-in-law Bill Skilling.

At the trial, Sir Redmond Barry sentenced Ellen Kelly to three years' hard labour. On the same charge, he sentenced Bricky and Bill to six years' hard labour. The jailing of his mother outraged Ned. He and Dan had headed for the hills after the incident in the kitchen. They hid out in the Wombat Ranges, where they set up a gold-mining camp and a whisky still to raise money for their mother's legal costs.

They also offered to give themselves up if their mother was released. Instead, the police set out to find – and kill, as some of the police had publicly promised – the Kelly brothers.

On 25 October, a party of four police, disguised as prospectors, camped at Stringybark Creek, close to where the Kelly boys had their hide-out. Two friends, Joe Byrne and Steve Hart, were with Ned and Dan when, the next day, they discovered the police camp and set out to disarm them and take their horses. Two of the troopers were relaxing around the campfire when the four emerged, and Ned barked: 'Bail up! Throw up your hands!' One of the troopers, McIntyre, surrendered immediately, but Constable Lonigan, a man who had once 'blackballed' Ned (grabbed and dragged him by the testicles), dived behind a log and came up gun in hand. Ned had once promised: 'If I ever shoot a man, Lonigan, you'll be the first!' As Lonigan raised his head, Ned shot him in the eye. Crying 'Oh Christ, I'm shot!', Lonigan fell dead across the log.

Now the Kelly boys and friends waited for the other two policemen. When Sergeant Kennedy and Constable Scanlon rode back into the campsite, they were met by McIntyre who told them, as Ned had ordered, that they had better surrender as they were surrounded. Scanlon laughed at the joke. His laughter died suddenly when Ned stepped out and called, 'Bail up! Hold your hands up!' As the other three members of the gang ran out calling on the police to bail up, Scanlon swung the barrel of his Spencer carbine and fired at Ned. Ned shot him off his horse, and Dan, probably, fired the shot that killed him. Kennedy had rolled off his horse and McIntyre sprang on it and rode for his life. Kennedy, firing as he went, followed on foot, dodging behind trees and reloading as he went. Ned came after him and shot him. Kennedy, Kelly considered, was mortally wounded, and he shot him again to finish him.

'I put his cloak over him,' Ned later said, 'and left him as well as I could and were they my own brothers I could not be more sorry for them. This cannot be called wilful murder for I was compelled to shoot them or lie down and let them shoot me. It would not be wilful murder if they packed our remains in, shattered into an animated mass of gore to Mansfield. They would have got great praise and credit . . . Certainly their wives and children are to be pitied, but they must remember those men came into the bush with the intention of scattering pieces of me and my brother all over the bush.'

With the deaths at Stringybark Creek, the Kelly Gang was born – four outlaws, with a price on their heads.

Six weeks later, with the colony still in ferment, the Kelly Gang pulled off their first, audacious hold-up. On the outskirts of the small town of Euroa, on the road to Sydney, the Kelly Gang invaded the Faithfull Creek homestead and locked up the station hands, a passing hawker, a selector and his son and others. Ned talked for hours to his captive audience about his life and the Mansfield Murders, as the shootout at Stringybark was now known. Some of the hostages slept, others stayed awake absorbed by his account, and some, sympathetic, offered him money, not knowing the gang was about to get their hands on a fortune very shortly.

The next morning, the gang cut the telegraph lines, burned their clothes and changed into new suits from the hawker's wagon. That afternoon, they bailed up another nine men, locked them with the others at the homestead under Joe's guard and went into Euroa's drowsy Binnie Street. At 4pm, Ned walked into the National Bank. Steve and Dan came in through the back. They bailed up the manager, Mr Scott and, after taking £2000, had so put him at ease that he shared a whisky with them. Scott was later to give evidence at Ned's trial that Ned was a gentleman and treated Mrs Scott well. The manager's wife was even more impressed. She told the police that Ned was 'a much more handsome and well dressed man than she had expected and by no means the ferocious ruffian she had expected him to be'.

Mr and Mrs Scott, along with her mother, nanny, maid, baby and younger children, were taken for a buggy ride that ended back at the Faithfull Creek homestead. By now the audience had now grown to 37 men, women and children, and the gang treated them to an exhibition of trick riding before departing, warning them not to go for help for three hours. One of the admiring audience reported:

> The horsemanship displayed by Ned Kelly is something surprising. He maintains his seat in the saddle in any position, sometimes resting his legs at full length along the horse's neck, and at others, extending his whole body till his toes rested on the tail, dashing along at full speed.

It was a hold-up that had hurt no-one and entertained all. 'The bushrangers,' noted the Melbourne *Herald*, 'played with the women and boys and treated everyone with the greatest civility.' The government, however, was not amused. It increased the reward for the gang's capture to £1000 dead or alive.

Eight weeks later, across the border, the Kelly Gang held the town of Jerilderie captive for two days and took another £2000 from the Bank of New South Wales. Once again, the event was cavalier and clever – this time the gang bailed up the entire town, including the police, stayed two days and left a lasting impression that, almost all agreed, was admirable. Ned, looking splendid in a police uniform, encountered the bank manager in his bath, bought drinks for the bar, made menacing boasts and showed his superb horsemanship. One of his captors, Constable Richards, said, 'He was the gamest man I ever saw.' And, another, who heard him make blood-chilling threats, noted, 'It was only a matter of bluff... from first to last.'

Ned came to Jerilderie with a written manifesto, 8300 words he had dictated to Joe Byrne, a virtual history that rambled and ranted in many places, but which succinctly explained his side of the story of Stringybark. He wanted the letter to be published, but like an earlier version he had written at Euroa, it was kept from public knowledge.

The Kelly Gang then disappeared for four months. Despite the most intensive police operation ever mounted in the colony, rounding up and jailing Kelly sympathisers, putting their houses under close watch and bringing Aboriginal trackers from Queensland the gang could not be found. While they laid low, the gang forged suits of armour from plough steel, inspired, it is conjectured, by a Chinese warrior's suit of armour they would have seen in Beechworth's Burke Museum (where it can still be seen), or perhaps by an armour-clad character in *Lorna Doon*, the then popular novel about an outlaw family in the late 17th century.

Above all, Ned and the gang spent this time planning a spectacular uprising one that would change the map of the British Empire. The uprising, Ned fantasised, would result in the establishment of a Republic in the north-east of the state – something he had forecast in the Jerilderie Letter: 'to show some colonial stratagem which will open the eyes not only of the Victoria police and its inhabitants but also the whole British Army'.

While the Kelly Gang eluded the police, Aaron Sherritt, a close friend of Joe, had been working as a double agent, informing the gang and the police of their respective movements, but always managing to keep the police one step behind. It was a dangerous business. When, finally, Joe Byrne suspected that his best mate had turned traitor, he shot Aaron at the door of his home while three police, there to guard Sherritt, cowered under the bed. Knowing that the killing of Aaron would bring a trainload of police to the murder site, Ned held up the tiny town of Glenrowan and got some railway-plate layers out of bed to tear up the railway line. The train would be derailed, the police would be killed, injured or unable to defend themselves and his supporters would fall on them. The north-east republican uprising would begin.

The train did set out, but not until 30 hours had passed. The police under the bed had been too frightened to leave the hut and raise the alarm. In the meantime, the Kelly Gang, in their fashion, had rounded up the townspeople many of them sympathisers and entertained them with a party at the Glenrowan Inn that went on until the early hours of Monday, 28 June 1880. It bore all the Kelly trademarks – generosity, civility, wild threats and songs and dance.

Then, as the police train neared Glenrowan, it was stopped by the local schoolteacher, Thomas Curnow, a man whom Ned, believing that he was a sympathiser, had released a few hours earlier. The police and their horses poured out of the train carriages and took up positions around the hotel. The Kelly Gang's last stand was at hand. Within the first few minutes of a pitched gun battle, Ned had wounded an old adversary, Superintendent Hare, but in return and despite his armour he had been badly wounded. He struggled on to Music, Joe's horse, got through the inadequate police cordon and went to warn his supporters that the plan had failed. Then he went back, coming in behind the pub just as a volley of shots hit Joe in the groin and he fell dying. Ned called for Steve and Dan to follow him. In the confusion, Ned went out alone and, in the bush, weak from loss of blood, passed out.

Just before dawn, Ned came to, got to his feet and made one last attempt to rescue Dan and Steve, trapped inside the inn. In the early morning mist, his helmeted figure, towering and black, emerged shooting at the cordon of police and taunting them: 'Good shots, boys. Fire away, you buggers, you cannot hurt me!' The truth was they *had* hurt him; he was reeling and staggering like a drunken man. Then Joe's horse, Music, saddled and bridled, came up to Ned from the trees. Kneeling by now, Ned let Music pass and she was shot.

Finally, it was over for Ned. After 30 minutes, the gunfight ended when he was brought down, close to death, with 28 bullet wounds. A Catholic priest, Dean Matthew Gibney, heard Ned's confession and, believing he was near death, gave him the last sacraments. Inside the inn, now set ablaze, Ned's mates were indeed dead. Father Gibney, showing incredible bravery, went into the burning building and came out as it was about to collapse, announcing: 'They're all dead!' Joe's body was dragged from the flames, but those of Steve and Dan were burnt beyond recognition. A young boy and two men had also died in the siege, fatally wounded by police bullets.

On 28 October 1880, at Melbourne's Supreme Court, Edward Kelly went to trial, charged with murdering Constable Thomas Lonigan at Stringybark Creek. He told his lawyer, David Gaunson:

> All I want is a full and fair trial and a chance to make my side heard. Until now the police have had all the say, and have had it all their own way.
>
> If I get a full and fair trial, I don't care how it goes; but I know this – the public will see that I was hunted and hounded on from step to step; they will see that I am not the monster I have been made out. What I have done has been under strong provocation.

The truth of Ned's comments emerged the following year at the Royal Commission into the police called as a result of the Kelly affair. Superintendent Nicholson admitted that the police had instructions that they 'should endeavour, whenever they commit any paltry crime, to bring [the Kellys] to justice and send them to Pentridge even on a paltry sentence, the object being to take their prestige away from them'.

Ned Kelly may have wanted a fair trial, but the counsel who represented him, Bindon, failed to ensure it. Bindon called no evidence on Kelly's behalf, stopped the Jerilderie Letter from being admitted as evidence and advised Ned not to give sworn evidence, or even an unsworn statement. In doing so, he brought the question of guilt down to one man's word. McIntyre, who had escaped the shootout at Stringybark, would tell the jury that Kelly shot Lonigan in cold blood, denying that Lonigan had raised his head from behind a log and was about to take aim when he was shot.

But would it have mattered? The trial was before Sir Redmond Barry, the Irish-born Protestant, a renowned hanging judge who had sentenced Ellen Kelly, Ned's mother, to three years' hard labour. At that time, it was later said, Barry told her and the court that he regretted that her son was not in the dock alongside her. 'I'd have given him 21 years.' Now he had her son before him. And, said John H Phillips, former chief justice of Victoria, in his book, *The Trial of Ned Kelly*, 'The conclusion is inescapable that Edward Kelly was not afforded a trial according to law.'

Kelly had always claimed he shot Lonigan and the other police at Stringybark in self-defence. 'It is all very well to say that we shot the police in cold blood. We had to do it in self defence,' he told John Tarleton, the Jerilderie bank manager. And, in the letter he handed over at Jerilderie he said:

> He [Lonigan] had just got to the logs and put his head up to take aim when I shot him that instant or he would have shot

me as I took him for Strahan the man who said he would not ask me to stand he would shoot me first like a dog.

...This cannot be called wilful murder for I was compelled to shoot them or lie down and let them shoot me... Remember these men came into the bush with the intention of scattering pieces of me and my brother all over the bush.

[The police parties had gone into the Wombat Ranges in search of Ned and Dan disguised as prospectors. Their horses carried long and stout straps to carry bodies out of the bush. And some had boasted that if it came to bringing the brothers back dead or alive they'd opt for the latter option.]

Nonetheless, Barry directed the jury to find Ned Kelly guilty or not guilty on the charge of murdering Lonigan and would not allow them to consider returning a finding of manslaughter – a verdict that would have agreed that Kelly had killed in self-defence. This ruling, that the jury could not consider a verdict of manslaughter, was plainly wrong, Justice John Phillips has said. Sir Redmond Barry, Phillips said, 'should have told the jury that it was for them to decide whether the police [at Stringybark Creek] were acting as ministers of justice or summary executioners' and 'should then have reviewed for the jurors the evidence relative to this issue. Instead the matter was put to the jury in terms that were conclusive in favour of the Prosecution . . . Whether the result would have been any different had the jury been correctly directed is, of course, entirely another matter.'

Without the possibility of considering a verdict of manslaughter, the jury took just 30 minutes to find Kelly guilty of Lonigan's murder. When Sir Redmond came to pronounce the death sentence, he was intensely nettled when Kelly argued that the charge of murder was false. But, Kelly conceded, the way that the evidence was presented meant the jury had no choice other than to find him guilty. It was his fault. 'It is not that I fear death; I fear it as little as to drink a cup of tea . . . I do not blame anybody neither Mr Bindon nor Mr Gaunson: but Mr Bindon knew nothing about my case. I lay blame on myself that I did not get up yesterday and examine the witnesses, but I thought that if I did so, it would look like bravado and flashness, and people might have said that I thought myself cleverer than Counsel. So I let it go as it was.'

In a famous exchange in which Kelly clearly got the better of the judge, he said, 'A day will come at a bigger court than this when we shall see which is right and which is wrong.' Then Sir Redmond pronounced that Edward Kelly would be taken 'to a place of execution, and there you will be hanged by the neck until you are dead. May the Lord have mercy on your soul.' And that should have been the last word. Ned, however, came back with, 'I'll go further than that, and say I will see you there where I go,' and two weeks after the hanging the judge suddenly died.

The date for the execution was set for 11 November 1880. In that short time – 13 days after the verdict of guilty – a petition for clemency went around Melbourne. The city's population was 300,000. More than one in 10 signed it, a phenomenal figure, pro rata, which has probably never been matched. (Unofficial figures for the petitions that came in too late put the total at above 60,000.) Four thousand people packed a public meeting at the Hippodrome and another 2000 to 3000 massed in the street outside. In today's terms, these figures would translate to a petition signed by 300,000 and a mass meeting of around 60,000 to 70,000 – a respectable figure for a modern-day football final. It was 'humiliating,' said one newspaper, 'to have to admit that a great number of respectable working people were present.'

The petition's appeal for a reprieve was rejected by the Governor, and on the day before Ned was to die, his mother, Ellen, said goodbye to her eldest son. She was brought from her wing of the jail, where she was still serving her sentence in the prison laundry. Traditionally, she is said to have told Ned, 'Mind you die like a Kelly, son,' but Ian Jones believes it far more likely that she said, 'I mind you'll die like a Kelly, son.' Ned also farewelled his brother Jim and his sisters, Kate and Grace, that day.

On the evening of 10 November 1880, Ned Kelly enjoyed his last meal – roast lamb with green peas and a bottle of claret – softly sang hymns and such songs as 'The Sweet Bye and Bye' and slept soundly till 5am, when he got up, went down on his knees and prayed silently for 20 minutes. Then he went back to sleep. He awoke at 8am, and the blacksmith came to take off his leg irons. Escorted from across the prison yard, Ned passed the cart waiting to take his corpse but simply nodded at some flowers growing by the wall. 'What beautiful flowers,' he said.

At the Melbourne Gaol, Ned was taken into a small holding cell a few metres from the gallows and given Extreme Unction, the church's solemn last rite, by Dean O'Hea, the priest who had baptised him as newborn, 26 years before. Then Upjohn the hangman, a huge, forbidding brute, pinioned his arms. 'There is no need for tying me,' Ned said. Unperturbed, Upjohn put a canvas hood on his head and, preceded by three priests and an acolyte, Ned walked the few steps to the gallows. He is said to have sighed: 'Ah, well, I suppose it had to come to this.' Then Upjohn slipped the noose around his neck, Ned shifting his head to make sure the knot was below his chin, and dropped the canvas cap over Ned's face. Almost in the same movement, the hangman sprang back and pulled the lever to the trapdoor.

'Death must have been instantaneous, beyond a slight twisting of the shoulders and spasmodic quiver of the larger limbs, no motion was visible,' an observer later recorded.

Ellen Kelly was cared for until her death in 1923 by her son Jim, the last of her 11 children. As a 14-year-old, Jim had been jailed for three years for the theft of four cattle. That term in prison stopped him becoming a member of the Kelly Gang. When Kate died in 1898 – she was found drowned – Ellen and Jim raised her three children. Ellen Kelly, the diminutive matriarch, tough as iron bark, who held the family together, lived on and died, a well-respected woman, at the age of 90. Jim Kelly died 23 years later, in 1946. He was 87.

The legend of Ned Kelly, however, lives on.

AZARIA CHAMBERLAIN

We all knew – well, most of us knew – that she was guilty; Lindy Chamberlain, the mother of the missing nine-week-old baby girl, Azaria. Lindy had said her baby was carried off by a dingo at their tourist camp site at Ayers Rock – Uluru, as it is now called – on 17 August 1980. We all knew – well, most of us knew – that wasn't the case and that Lindy Chamberlain had killed Azaria with the help of her husband Michael.

Australia was riveted by the case, and the world watched it with some bemusement. What intrigued Australians was the demeanour of Azaria's parents. But what fascinated all, those who followed every minute detail of the story in Australia and those around the world whose curiosity was aroused, were the circumstances and the setting. A dingo, you say? And at Ayers Rock?

Had the Chamberlains been holidaying anywhere else in the Australian Outback the case, though sensational – 'A dingo has taken my baby!' – would not have gripped the nation. The dramatic back-drop of 'the Rock', however, turned the story into a drama watched globally.

Lindy Chamberlain and her husband Michael, undeniably, were a curious couple. On the night of the disappearance of Azaria and in the days after, their reactions to the gruesome fate of their baby seemed bizarre. When almost all the camp site near Ayers Rock went into the night searching for Azaria, Lindy and Michael stayed at the site, incomprehensible behaviour to those whose maternal and paternal instinct would be to run into the darkness screaming the name of their child in the forlorn hope of hearing a pitiful answering cry. A few days later, Michael, a photography enthusiast, rang the Melbourne *Sun News-Pictorial* and asked if the newspaper would like to publish his shots of Ayers Rock. And on leaving the place where a dingo had trotted off into the darkness carrying their little girl in its jaws they stopped to buy souvenir coffee mugs bearing images of the Rock.

In Alice Springs court, Lindy continued to confound. She seemed unmoved as the prosecution introduced a parade of forensic experts who testified that it was likely that the baby's throat had been cut, probably with scissors, and that a spray of foetal blood had been found in the couple's Holden Torana.

Damning, expert, evidence. But most damning was the circumstantial 'evidence': the detached demeanour of Lindy, as we all called her. A Seventh Day Adventist, she looked anything but. She pouted, she seemed sulky, almost sultry. She appeared at court each day wearing fresh outfits that might have been chosen for their effect on the camera crews who jostled outside the courthouse. (Some journalists at the trial admitted to being affected. One had a mild crush on her.)

Lindy Chamberlain just didn't look or act the way we expected a grieving mother on trial for the murder of her daughter would act. But there were those who staunchly believed in her innocence. 'Bastards!' reporter Malcolm Brown yelled – not showing the demeanour or acting in the way we expect of journalists – when the jury brought in its verdict of guilty.

And then in January 1986, police investigating the death of a British tourist near the Rock found the little matinee jacket that Lindy had claimed Azaria was wearing when she disappeared. The jacket had tooth marks. Doubts about Lindy Chaberlain's guilt began to gather.

Sixteen months later a Royal Commission began looking afresh at the evidence that had sent Lindy Chamberlain to jail for life. This time forensic experts called by Lindy's barrister told the commission that what had been alleged to be a bloody adult handprint on the baby's jumpsuit had in fact been nothing more than red sand; that the blood in the car was sound deadener and sealant, standard in Holden cars.

In 1988, Lindy Chamberlain successfully appealed against her conviction. The Northern Territory Government paid her $1.3 million in compensation and we all agreed – well, most of us, anyway – that we had always known her to be innocent. It always had been a disgraceful miscarriage of justice.

In the following decade, when John Bryson wrote *Evil Angels*, his forensic dissection of the case and its forensic experts, the fault, we all agreed, lay with the 'experts' and with the rednecks of the Northern Territory who refused to believe that a dingo would carry off a baby, and certainly not at the sacred heart of the nation, the icon, Uluru, as we were now all happy to call it.

GUN ALLEY and the Man Fit to be Hanged

There they were. The strands of hair that had hanged Colin Campbell Ross.

Kevin Morgan opened the faded blue envelope at Melbourne's Public Record Office. It was August 1995. He had, with some reluctance, been given a box of documents, legal briefs and testimonies. From the box he took the envelope and opened it.

What he saw inside stunned him – three samples of hair: one belonging to 12-year-old murdered schoolgirl, Alma Tirtschke; another from a blanket belonging to Colin Ross; and the third from Ross's girlfriend. They had been in the envelope for 73 years – the only piece of physical evidence connecting Colin Ross to Alma Tirtschke's murder, but enough to hang him.

'Just before she was buried, the two policeman went out to her home and as she lay in her coffin they cut from her head a lock of her hair,' Kevin Morgan told the ABC's *PM* radio program.

'Two weeks later they arrested Colin Campbell Ross and they took from him some blankets and on those blankets they found some hairs and they had the government chemist of the day have a look at those hairs and he was willing to testify in court at Colin Ross's trial that these hairs, and I quote, "come from the scalp of one and the same person".'

Discovering the hair samples, Kevin Morgan may have felt much the same emotion as did Howard Carter when the archaeologist uncovered the tomb of Tutankhamen in 1922 – the same year Colin Ross hanged. For both men the discoveries came after years of meticulous digging – forensic, in ʻevin Morgan's case. Both were astonished by their unexpected success. Howard Carter had found a fabulous ancient burial tomb. Kevin Morgan's find was much more prosaic: sad strands of hair that were the macabre answer to the question of Colin Ross's guilt. But, Kevin Morgan knew, they would resolve a question that had been argued over for eight decades: was Colin Ross a killer, or was he a victim of a disgraceful travesty of justice?

The murder of Alma Tirtschke inspired the artist Charles Blackman in the 1950s to create *Schoolgirls and Angels*, a series of disturbing paintings. Some of the paintings depicted a young girl, her face always hidden, hurrying somewhere in her school tunic and a straw hat, like the uniform Alma was wearing before she was raped and strangled. In 1993, the National Gallery of Victoria held a retrospective exhibition of the paintings. Kevin Morgan, who was working as a trainee librarian at the gallery, was intrigued by them and their history. He began to read newspapers of the time; he went on to study public documents and, eventually, to contact the relatives of those main figures in the puzzle.

He became so absorbed by the case that he gave up his job and, supported by his wife, embarked on a long and meticulous search for the truth, a search he documented in *Gun Alley: Murder, Lies and Failure of Justice*.

It is a story that began late on the morning of New Year's Eve, 1921, when a bottle-o – collecting empty bottles for resale – found 12-year-old Alma Tirtschke's naked body in Gun Alley, a back lane off Little Collins Street in the heart of Melbourne.

Within a fortnight, 28-year-old Colin Campbell Ross, the owner of a failed and seedy wine saloon, was on trial for her murder. The prosecution claimed that he'd lured Alma into his saloon, got her drunk, then raped and strangled her before carrying her body, in a blanket, to Gun Alley.

It took just five days for the jury to find Ross guilty. Ross appealed to a higher court, lost, and appealed again and lost. Less than four months after the murder, Ross died an agonising death that may have taken as long as 20 minutes, hanged from the same scaffold that Ned Kelly had swung from in 1880.

Colin Ross was no angel. The year before the murder he had been in a lovers' quarrel —melodramatically confronting his girlfriend of two years, Lily May Brown, and insisting that they get married that day. Lily declined. But to emphasise his proposal Ross drew a revolver, and said he would have her dead or alive. Put that way it was hard for Lily to say no, and she agreed to meet him that evening. When she did, she had a policeman with her. Arrested and at the watch house, Ross was found to have a loaded revolver and a gold ring in his pockets. He was fined and put on a 12-month good-behaviour bond. Later, in October 1921, only months before the murder, Ross was acquitted of 'rolling' a drunk in the lavatory outside his wine bar. It was that kind of a wine bar.

Ivy Matthews, a barmaid at the wine bar and the prosecution's main witnesses against Ross – she told the court he had confessed to her – said, 'During Colin Ross's tenancy of the wine café, I came into contact with all kinds of men, including thieves and fences. These men gave me their confidences, and I have never broken them. I used to have a very narrow outlook on life . . . My experience in the wine bar had been a great education.'

Like many things she said, her 'narrow outlook on life' was far from the truth. She was a prostitute, an inveterate liar and an abortionist.

The facts about Alma Tirtschke's murder, however, will be

forever blurred by contradictory evidence and the desperation of the Crown and the media to convict someone – anyone. Some, few, facts are not in dispute. Alma, a girl who topped her class and was quiet and well-behaved, was last seen in Little Collins Street, standing outside the Adam and Eve boarding house, a place known to be used by prostitutes. She was on an errand for her auntie.

Reliable witnesses – few of the Crown witnesses could be relied on: they included two street walkers, a fortune teller and a criminal, all rewarded for their testimony against Ross – said the girl looked anxious and frightened, as if she was being followed. One said he saw a man – not Ross – persistently following her and then talking to her. The time, all agreed, was between 2.30 and 3 pm.

Ross was known to be inside his wine bar, the Australian Wine Shop, in the Eastern Arcade, for the entire afternoon. He freely admitted that he had seen a girl like Alma pass his saloon, 'as if she was looking for somebody . . . She had a black skirt, it was pleated; and a white hat. She was a college girl. There was a band on her hat with red . . . Her hair was golden coloured and hung down her back.'

A cab driver, Joseph Graham, told police, 'I was walking slowly up Little Collins Street . . . It was between a quarter and half past three. I was opposite . . . the Adam and Eve Hotel. I heard a piercing scream, followed immediately by others; terrifying screams . . . I heard at least five screams – more like six – then the girl seemed to be exhausted . . . they seemed to be at the back of the Adam and Eve Hotel. They were . . . like a little girl terrified at what was occurring or about to occur. I reported it to the detective office.'

Joseph Graham was not called to give evidence. His account didn't fit the chain of events the police had constructed.

Another witness, who gave evidence to the police but, like Graham, was not called, corroborated much of his story. George Crilley had been questioned by the police several times and when he was not called, approached the Ross family. At his appeal Ross's barrister sought to produce this new evidence from Crilley – who said he had seen a girl who looked like Alma Tirtschke walking up Little Collins Street with a man walking just behind her. The man appeared to be following her so Crilley was going to speak to him but then the man walked past her. When Crilley looked back he saw the man talking to Alma.

The Chief Justice refused to hear Crilley but said the court would consider his statement.

The police, the politicians and the judiciary wanted the murderer punished, and to that end evidence was manipulated and suppressed. In 1961, Detective Inspector Piggott remembered, '. . . the public were clamouring for police action and the politicians of course were harassing us . . . But we survived the uproar long enough to plump for the theory that Ross ravished and strangled Alma in the saloon . . . Bur we were well aware that our evidence . . . was only circumstantial.'

So the police had chosen – plumped for – a theory. All they had to do was find a man who would fit it. The clincher, the evidence that sent Colin Ross to the gallows, were the hair samples on two blankets belonging to Ross that had been taken from his home. Charles Price, the government analyst – a chemist who had virtually no experience examining hairs – told the court he had put 27 hairs from the blankets under a microscope and compared them with a dozen hairs taken from the lock cut from Alma's head as she lay in her coffin. The hairs from the blanket were not identical in colour to Alma's, they were a different diameter, and had probably 'cast off in the ordinary process of nature'. There were semen stains on one blanket. (Ross had girlfriends.) In short, you might think, the government analyst would tell the court that the hairs on the blanket were not Alma's. That was not Charles Price's conclusion. He found that the hair samples on the blanket and from Alma 'were derived from the scalp of one and the same person'. With those words he doomed Colin Ross.

But if Colin Ross was not the murderer, who was? In *Gun Alley: Murder, Lies and Failure of Justice,* Kevin Morgan mounts a powerful case that the killer was a close relative of the Tirtschke family, George Murphy, a disturbed war veteran with distinct paedophilic tendencies and a history of pestering Alma's sister Viola. Morgan believes that Murphy was the man seen following and talking to the frightened Alma.

Before he died on 24 April 1922, Ross wrote to his family telling them the day would come when he would be proved innocent. That day came. But it took 88 years. And it came only because of the amateur detective work of Kevin Morgan. In 1998, Morgan won a legal fight for the right to submit the hair samples he had discovered for DNA testing. Dr Bentley Atchison of the Victoria Institute of Forensic Medicine found that the hairs did not come from the same person. Then the Australian Federal Police tested the hairs and confirmed the finding.

Three senior Victorian judges found Ross had suffered a miscarriage of justice and he was posthumously pardoned.

Victoria's Attorney General Rob Hulls said, 'We are repairing a wrong in this state's history. I hope that the pardon does go some way in making amends for the tragedy that befell both families.'

It was a pardon. Not an exoneration. Colin Ross surely deserved that.

THE DEBATABLE

Having strong points on both sides that can be questioned or disputed

MEN AT WORK and the Down Under Plunder

Do you come from a land Down Under?
Where women glow and men plunder?

— Men at Work, 'Down Under'

It had a little of ska, a little of reggae and a lot of Australia, the song that in 1983 topped the charts – Number One single and Number One album – in Australia, the US and the UK. But in 2010, a judge found it had more than that: it had a flute riff based on the tune of another famous Australian song, the children's jingle 'Kookaburra Sits in the Old Gum Tree'.

Written by Melbourne teacher Marion Sinclair for a Girl Guides jamboree in 1934, 'Kookaburra Sits in the Old Gum Tree' is wired into the musical memory bank of generations of Australian children. It's a pleasant memory and one that Justice Peter Jacobsen ruled Men at Work had summoned when they wrote 'Down Under'. He ordered Men at Work frontman Colin Hay, his fellow songwriter Ron Strykert and EMI to pay Larrikin Music, the company that had the rights to 'Kookaburra', five per cent of future profits, as well as royalties dating back to 2002.

It was a ruling greeted with almost universal rancour. Both

songs were part of the Australian psyche. 'Kookaburra' is the children's classic. 'Down Under' is our unofficial anthem. It played – defiantly – from our triumphant America's Cup yacht, *Australia II*, as she sailed out to do battle for the trophy in 1983. Men at Work forgot their acrimony and re-formed to perform it, memorably, at the closing ceremony of the Sydney Olympics. It was on Paul Hogan's *Kangaroo Jack* soundtrack, it was on the trailer for *Finding Nemo* and more than 30 years on since it was composed, 'Down Under', internationally, has surpassed 'Waltzing Matilda' as Australia's signature song.

If, as Larrikin Music claimed, and Justice Jacobsen agreed, it had plagiarised a few bars of 'Kookaburra' what did it matter? It was, unconsciously or not, a reference, one of a number of references that struck a chord (no pun intended) with Australians; references that made us immensely proud of the larrikin in us (a word that is, ironically, part of the name of the company that sued for damages). To write a song celebrating Vegemite sandwiches, swearing women and vomiting men, as Hay and Styrkert did, isn't easy. To see it embraced worldwide, Australian esoteric references or not, and then to have a few bars of flute motif damned as plagiarism seemed to most of us to be, well, un-Australian.

Colin Hay commented:

> It is no surprise that in over 20 years, no-one noticed the reference to 'Kookaburra'. There are reasons for this. It was inadvertent, naive, unconscious, and by the time Men at Work recorded the song, it had become unrecognisable . . . When I co-wrote 'Down Under' back in 1978, I appropriated nothing from anyone else's song. There was no Men at Work, there was no flute, yet the song existed.
>
> That's the truth of it, because I was there; Norm Lurie [Larrikin Music] was not, and neither was Justice Jacobson. 'Down Under' lives in my heart, and may perhaps live in yours.

It certainly lived in the hearts of a diverse audience.

The song has been appropriated by Jewish wedding bands. 'Apparently,' says Colin Hay, 'it has a very similar structure to a lot of Jewish folk songs.' In South Korea, the song was a favourite because words like Vegemite and chunder somehow sounded Korean.

Elsewhere, from Podunk, Connecticut to Miles End, England, the curious Australianisms bothered no-one. They simply liked the song, no matter what it meant.

JIM and JUNI and the Love that – Finally – Spoke Its Name

It was 1975. Derryn Hinch, then editor of the Sydney *Sun,* was in his office when Toni McRae, a reporter he admired for her passion and integrity, burst in. McRae told Hinch it was 'imperative' that he have lunch with a woman named Juni Morosi.

'I was aware of the exotic Eurasian beauty and her rumoured, powerful relationship with the former Deputy Prime Minister Jim Cairns,' Hinch said on the death of Cairns in 2003. 'I had been living in America at the height of the heady Cairns years and his leadership of the anti-American Vietnam War street demonstrations.

'Lunch with the sultry Morosi was intriguing. She turned up wearing sort of gaucho gear and a poncho. Later we were joined by her husband, David Ditchburn, who started to tell this total stranger about his wife's prehensile sexual talents.

'It was a bizarre lunch and to this day I do not know why we broke bread together. But it was in my newspaper that McRae broke the story – and I wrote the headline – about Jim Cairns and his "kind of love for Juni".'

George Negus on ABC TV in 2002 asked, 'Can you imagine

today's politics producing a scandal like the one that raged around one Juni Morosi? How can we describe Juni? A somewhat exotic staffer in the old 1972–75 cowboy days of the Whitlam government. Along came Morosi and the press at the time had a field day.'

The press at the time did its best to describe Juni Morosi. The reports began somewhat timidly, Mike Gibson in 1974 describing her as 'an attractive 41-year-old Filipino lady'. Things hotted up when she became the first woman to take the position of Principal Private Secretary to a senior federal minister – the treasurer, Jim Cairns. South Australian political staffer Adele Koh complained irritably of the way the press treated Juni Morosi, 'The Australian press is still infantile . . . it does not know how to control its bowels. Only one paper has to get on to a good story and we get several cases of verbal and pictorial diarrhoea, all trying to go one better.'

'Glamour comes to treasury' said one headline and 'Juni – she's a real stunner' said another. 'She has a full, sensuous lower lip and an eye-catching dark spot, just right of centre on her upper lip . . . [She is] slim with the curves in the right places,' drooled the feature writer. The fact that she had mixed Asian blood – her Italian father and her Portuguese mother were both part-Chinese; she was born in Shanghai and educated in Manila – added to her exotic appeal: 'She has the high cheekbones of her Asian forebears,' an entranced reporter panted, 'and she walks with the in-born grace of the East.' Jim Cairns would agree with all of that.

He was 60 at the time. She was almost 20 years younger. They were both married, Jim to Gwen, since 1939, and Juni to her second husband, David Ditchburn, a businessman. Ditchburn's relationship with Juni was intriguing. It was Ditchburn, who, after the tape-recorder was switched off, suggested to reporter Toni McRae in an interview with Juni and Jim in 1975 at which he was also present, that McRae ask Cairns one more question: 'Do you love Juni Morosi?'

Jim and Juni and the Love that – Finally – Spoke Its Name 235

Cairns responded: 'Love is a word that has many meanings. I would like to add, though, that in her capacity as my private secretary, Juni must command my respect and trust. Surely you can't trust somebody in this world unless you feel something akin to a kind of love for them.'

Hinch had his headline.

The Jim and Juni affair – 'MY LOVE FOR Juni' the *Sun*'s headline was accompanied by a photograph of Morosi in a swimsuit – confirmed what all but the most gullible Australians had by now assumed. The front-page photographs told the story: Jim Cairns, the treasurer, the man respected by millions for his quiet, calm integrity, was shown with his chest bare, leading Juni Morosi by the hand, with a faint whiff of the caveman and his conquest. Juni looked smug and Jim had the 'gee shucks' smile of a lovesick schoolboy. Prime Minister Gough Whitlam put it bluntly: 'Jim is c----struck,' he privately told colleagues.

'Jim and Juni were attracted to each other from the first time they met,' Labor's doughty old warrior Tom Uren, a minister in the Whitlam cabinet and one of Cairns's closest friends wrote. 'They shared my flat so I knew what was going on.'

Morosi's 'perception of relationships,' he wrote, 'was very different to what I had been used to. I remember her saying to me, "Tommy, you Anglo-Saxon men look at sex so differently to we Asians."'

Jim Cairns was an attractive man, handsome and athletic, but he may have been inhibited with women. When Morosi met him, he exhibited all the signs of a man besotted with a woman for perhaps the first time. His mother, Letitia, may have had much to do with Cairns's inhibitions. Tom Uren explained, 'He never saw his father [Cairns' father, a clerk, went to World War I, and for some reason never returned] but his mother, she was a wonderful mother, but she didn't show him affection and he found it very hard to show personal affection.'

In 1999, Cairns told SBS television that his mother had syphilis, contracted from her runaway husband, and was afraid of passing it on. He loved his mother and he believed she loved him, but this love never extended to hugs or kisses; the closest they came physically was to shake hands.

Morosi, clearly, awakened him sexually.

Juni Morosi was introduced to Jim Cairns by Lionel Murphy, the then Attorney General, who had met her through Al Grassby. She worked for both men. Mrs Murphy and Morosi's husband David Ditchburn were involved in a business relationship and Lionel Murphy had appointed Ditchburn to the Commonwealth Film Board.

Before coming to Australia, Morosi had worked for Qantas but her business background in the travel industry hardly equipped her to hold down the job as Cairns' Principal Private Secretary, a job traditionally held by a senior public servant. She controlled his appointment book, and Treasury and Labor colleagues were concerned that she was cutting out a lot of the people Cairns should have been seeing and admitting others, some rather dubious businessmen sent by her husband.

On 4 December 1974, a Liberal backbencher new to Parliament rose, 'somewhat reluctantly', he said, to bring Parliament's attention to 'a well publicised appointment to the staff of the future treasurer, the Deputy Prime Minister and Minister for Overseas trade, Dr JF Cairns'. The backbencher, John Howard, went on to say that he understood that Morosi and Ditchburn were 'directors, officers and/or shareholders' of companies the subject of investigation by the NSW Commissioner of Corporate Affairs.

'I raise this matter,' Howard said, 'because I know such a suggestion will prompt an immediate investigation by the Government.' Morosi resigned, but when the investigation found no irregularities, Cairns promptly re-appointed her and two months later, at the Labor Party's national conference at Terrigal, brought the media

Jim and Juni and the Love that – Finally – Spoke Its Name

circus to a climax when he told Toni McCrae that he felt a kind of love for her.

Five months after he talked of his feelings for his secretary, Whitlam sacked Cairns.

For a time, in the minds of some of the public, the 'kind of love' he had for Juni Morosi helped Cairns. But many wondered just what that kind of love was. Both denied any imputations that it was a carnal love – and sued those who suggested that it was.

In 2002 Jim Cairns, for some extraordinary reason and after 27 years of denial, cleared up the matter in a radio interview with the ABC's John Cleary. Why? It seems very likely that in his last years he couldn't resist boasting.

> JIM CAIRNS: Yes, my point of popularity insofar as I've appeared in public opinion polls, was at the highest it had ever reached in April 1975 – that is after six months of Morosi publicity. My popularity rating was the highest it's ever been at 63 per cent.
>
> JOHN CLEARY: There's no such thing as bad publicity, I guess is what that is indicating.
>
> JIM CAIRNS: It wasn't bad. I don't think it was. I don't think the ordinary person thought I was wrong or a fool in going to bed with Juni Morosi. They thought it was a pretty good thing ... [They thought] 'I'd have done the same.'
>
> JOHN CLEARY: Did you go to bed with Juni Morosi?
>
> JIM CAIRNS: Yes.
>
> JOHN CLEARY: That'll satisfy the public on certain matters. To what extent, then, was this affair one which became consuming for you – all-consuming?
>
> JIM CAIRNS: I don't know.
>
> JOHN CLEARY: See, many of your colleagues said you were profoundly distracted by the whole thing.
>
> JIM CAIRNS: I was quite distracted. I don't know whether the

word profound is fair. It distracted me quite a lot, yes. I think the distraction in a way led to events happening that allowed Whitlam to sack me... I think the Morosi affair gave him much reason to believe that he would get away with it. He sacked me for reasons that I don't think under – in any way – are very significant. As a matter of fact I'm not quite sure what they were.

Jim Cairns died the following year.

The biggest sex scandal in Australia's political history played a powerful part in the downfall of the Whitlam government and many in the Labor Party shared the feelings expressed by the *Sydney Morning Herald*'s Alan Ramsey, though no-one expressed them so viciously. 'There was always more myth than reality about Jim Cairns, an evangelist at his best as an oppositionist and pursuer of great causes but who should never, ever have been allowed anywhere near government, let alone to become its second most senior figure. Cairns was a disgrace as a minister, despite all the after-death rhetorical slop.'

Paddy McGuiness, the editor of the conservative monthly *Quadrant*, was kinder. 'He was not a bad man, nor was there evil in his heart, if only he had been a pastor in a minor congregation where no-one noticed him he could have done some good.' And John Howard 'respected the strength and integrity of his views'.

Cairns' fall was sad. The once immensely respected figurehead of the anti-Vietnam War movement joined Morosi in a series of alternative lifestyle projects and espoused the bizarre sexual theories of the psychiatrist Wilhelm Reich. In 1985, Prime Minister Hawke intervened and wound up a 'community housing project' in which Morosi, Ditchburn and her brother and sister-in-law, were involved. Cairns had helped financially and the co-op also had a $133,000 federal grant. The next year Morosi went into hospital suffering from stress and Cairns was reconciled with his wife Gwen.

Jim and Juni and the Love that – Finally – Spoke Its Name

Following Gwen's death, Jim Cairns was a familiar sight to shoppers at a card table at the entrances to Melbourne suburban markets. A shunned and lonely figure selling self-published books, he was barely recognisable as the heroic figure of the Vietnam moratoriums, the man who came very close to beating Whitlam to the leadership of the Labor Party.

Cairns' misfortune was to fall for a woman who seemed to wear a label: Sex Bomb. There were many men on both sides of politics in federal and state parliaments who had affairs at the same time, Bob Hawke, notoriously. Only Jim Cairns was exposed, vilified and ridiculed. But then, only Jim Cairns was foolish enough to put his mistress into a position of power where she could, and did, cause real damage to him and his party. And only Jim Cairns sued for defamation knowing that his case was false.

In 1982, in the Supreme Court of New South Wales, Jim Cairns and Juni Morosi brought a defamation case against the *National Times* over an interview with an American director of financiers Morgan Stanley, who referred to Cairns's 'girlfriend Morosi'. Cairns said that this implied that he was 'improperly involved with his assistant, Juni Morosi, in a romantic or sexual association contrary to the obligations of his marriage and to that of Miss Morosi'.

Juni told the jury of four men: 'I felt insulted, angry, upset and hurt. It was very demeaning to me as a woman [to be called a "girlfriend"]. I saw myself as a professional, as a competent person doing her job. It was cheap. It was as though it had nothing to do with business but everything to do with sex.'

The jury found that the imputation did arise from the article in the *National Times*, but that it was not defamatory. Jim and Juni appealed, saying that the jury's finding was 'perverse', but lost.

Juni had earlier sued the *Mirror* and was awarded $17,000 for a number of defamatory publications, one of which was a cartoon which she said implied she had a 'romantic attachment with the

Treasurer, Dr Cairns'. And she had a further win in a defamation action against 2GB over a broadcast by Ormsby Wilkins, which, she pleaded, deliberately imputed that she was 'an undesirable, immoral and promiscuous woman who had misconducted herself with her employer, Dr Jim Cairns'. The jury agreed and awarded Juni $10,000.

Jim Cairns died aged 89 in 2003 and was buried after a service at St John's Toorak, the church of choice for Melbourne's social set. Among the mourners were some of the Labor Party's great figures. Juni Morosi did not attend.

AGW and the History Wars. As One Cools, the Other Heats Up

It used to be a staple of cartoonists, the sketch, traditionally of a man in a toga and sandals (to make it clear that he was a nut case, and probably a vegetarian). The man is carrying a placard that reads: 'The End of the World is Nigh'. The caption always treated this as a humorous prediction.

You don't see that cartoon these days. That's because many people think the end of the world as we know it *is* nigh. And the man in the toga and sandals? Well, like climate alarmists such as Al Gore he makes a fortune flying around the world telling us to change our light bulbs, to drive hybrid cars, to close down coal mines and to put up wind turbines before it's all too late.

On the eve of the Copenhagen Climate Change Summit of 2009, we were told the Doomsday Clock was at one minute to midnight. Gordon Brown, the then prime minister of the United Kingdom, warned that there were fewer than 50 days to set the course of the next 50 years and that the world was on the brink of a 'catastrophic' future of killer heatwaves, floods and droughts.

The Prince of Wales was a little more relaxed. He warned that 'we have only 100 months left to take the necessary steps to avert irretrievable climate and ecosystem collapse'.

Closer to home, Tim Flannery, an expert in fossils and Australian of the Year in 2007, had earlier warned in 2008 that global warming could reduce Perth to a ghost city; that Adelaide could run out of water by 2009; that the Arctic could become ice-free; and that rising seas could reach the level of eight-storey buildings.

Australia's then prime minister Kevin Rudd and his colleagues were equally worried. Man-made global warming science was settled, they said. Mr Rudd's authority, he said, was 'the IPCC – the International Panel on Climate Change – 4000 essentially humourless scientists in white coats who go around and measure things'.

Mr Rudd got the IPCC's name wrong – it's the Intergovernmental Panel on Climate Change – and his version of what a scientist looks like, never mind their sense of humour or their method of working, seems to have been inspired by the same cartoonists who draw men in togas carrying placards. But worse, on the eve of the Copenhagen summit, more than 1000 leaked emails from the database of the University of East Anglia's Climatic Research Unit – the world's leading alarmist centre – revealed that the science was far from settled. Measurements were being manipulated.

Twelve months later, Brown and Rudd had gone and gone with them, it seemed, was the clear and present danger of global warming. By the end of 2010, it was a subject that Julia Gillard, Rudd's successor, seemed to be scrupulously avoiding.

There is another staple of the cartoonists of course: the man with the toga carrying a placard that reads 'Repent'. And at the same time as Prime Minister Gillard was no longer parroting 'the science is settled', another former prime minister was dashing off a vitriolic letter to the press over the ownership of his famous repentant Redfern Park Speech. Paul Keating claimed that while his speechwriter Don Watson may have 'authored' the speech, the sentiments in it were PJ Keating's.

Almost 20 years after he gave the speech in December 1992,

Keating's letter reminded us of its central theme: that 'we did the dispossessing ... we brought the diseases, the alcohol, that we committed the murders and took the children from their mothers'.

Like man-made climate change, the notion that the tragedy of the Australian Aborigines was white man-made became increasingly prevalent around the turn of the century. The day after the Sydney Olympics opened in 2000, the *New York Times* ran an editorial that said, 'The Aboriginal experience is depressingly similar to that of Native Americans in the United States. European settlers viciously drove the Aborigines from their land, massacring thousands with impunity.'

The editorial writer may have been influenced by the Australian expatriate Ben Kiernan, once a defender of Pol Pot's genocidal Khmer Rouge regime now Professor of History and head of the Genocide Studies Project at Yale University. In 2000, Kiernan wrote *Australia's Aboriginal Genocides*, in which he claimed Australian settlers had committed 'hundreds of massacres' and the Aborigines had been 'hunted like wild beasts, having lived for years in a state of absolute terror of white predators'.

That same year Phillip Knightley wrote in his *Australia – A Biography of a Nation* 'Australia was able to get away with a racist policy that included segregation and dispossession and slavery and genocide practices unknown in the civilized world until Nazi Germany turned on the Jews in the 1930s.'

Knightley put a figure on the number of Aborigines killed in the 'wars and massacres' of the past two centuries. 'Experts I have consulted say that 50,000 would not be an exaggeration. It could be as high as 100,000 ... It is amazing that Australians managed to keep from the rest of the world the fact that they were massacring the Aboriginals.' Indeed. A death toll of 100,000 would be more than the total number of Australians killed in both world wars.

John Pilger, the expatriate journalist, wrote, 'Few whites appreciate the legacy and scale of the genocide in Australia. While 10 per cent of Jewry died in the Holocaust, the great majority of the first Australians died in the onslaught of white invasion and appropriation. In 1987, a sensational "discovery" was made by a Sydney University team, led by Australia's most celebrated pre-historian, Professor DJ Mulvaney. They reported that the Australian population in 1788 was 750,000, or three times the previous estimate. They concluded that more than 600,000 people had died as result of white settlement.'

How accurate are those estimates, and how many of the deaths caused by white settlement – a toxic blend of introduced diseases, killings and neglect – can be attributed to 'genocide'?

In 2002, the historian Keith Windschuttle reported in his book *The Fabrication of Australian History* that in Tasmania, where the genocidal policy was said to have been enacted, the recorded number of Aborigines who died violently in the three decades between 1803 and 1834 – the height of the violence between Aborigines and settlers – was 120 according to his investigations. The Black Line campaign of 1830, said to be an early example of 'ethnic cleansing', cost a total of three Aboriginal lives. Only one trooper was killed by Aborigines in the history of Tasmania, Windschuttle says, belying the claims of the prominent historian Henry Reynolds that an Aboriginal guerrilla war waged against the whites was 'the biggest internal threat Australia has ever had'.

Most embarrassingly for Reynolds, noted for his books on the 'frontier wars', Windschuttle showed that the historian had grievously misquoted Governor Arthur on the question of the extermination – or otherwise – of the Aborigines of Van Diemen's Land. Reynolds had quoted Arthur as expressing in a letter his fears that conflict with the Aborigines would lead to 'eventual extirpation [total extermination] of the colony'. In fact, as Windschuttle showed, Governor Arthur, far from being concerned about the extermination of the European settlers (the colony) actually wrote of measures to prevent 'the extirpation of the aboriginal race itself'.

AGW and the History Wars. As One Cools, the Other Heats Up 245

Windschuttle doesn't dispute that other, unrecorded, killings may have occurred in Tasmania, nor can he ignore the depressing reality that within half a century from the time of European settlement there was not a single Aborigine left on the island. His quarrel is with those who he says have presented a grossly inaccurate picture of the conflict between the two races.

Windschuttle's findings relate only to Tasmania. But at the same time, the accounts of massacres by whites in Western Australia were looked at critically by a respected Perth journalist, Rod Moran. In his book *Massacre Myth*, Moran clinically investigated an alleged massacre and incineration of 100 Aborigines at Forrest River. He found that oral accounts of the massacre were first heard 50 years after it was said to have occurred. There were was no eyewitnesses and no forensic evidence of killings. And, he argued, to incinerate 100 bodies would need a mountain of wood – 225 tonnes.

Both Windschuttle and Moran assert that for decades some historians have fed us a diet that has supported claims of genocide and massacre. The 'history wars' ignited, one side dismissing Windschuttle and Moran as amateurs who had bumbled into an area of academia they knew nothing about, the other condemning the historians, who, they charged, allowed facts to wait upon ideology.

Have we been fed a twisted version of the truth about the clash between Aborigines and whites? Have we been given 'versions of the truth' as one historian insisted was legitimate. (Lyndall Ryan, when challenged by Windschuttle for inflating the number of Aborigines killed by white men responded: 'Historians are always making up figures.') Have we been fed facts fabricated, falsified, exaggerated, distorted or glossed over to suit those who propagate what Geoffrey Blainey called 'the black armband' view of our history?

Or, is it that, as academic Dr Dirk Moses claimed in 2005, 'Falsely accusing Australian historians of exaggerating claims of genocide and holocaust in Australia in order to paint them as ideologically driven is now common among history warriors.' Dr Moses, along the way, accused Windschuttle of 'castration anxiety'.

Five years earlier, before Keith Windschuttle's claims sparked the history wars, the same Dr Moses had written, 'Australia had many genocides, perhaps more than any other country', and Bain Attwood wrote about 'what can and should be called a holocaust given the scale of loss and the trauma that has been suffered'. In 2005, the same Bain Attwood contended, 'Windschuttle has not provided any evidence for his imputation that academic historians have compared the British colonisation of this country to Nazi Germany's treatment of Jews or caused others to make such a comparison. This is a figment of his imagination.'

The history wars have resulted, it would seem, in the end of the genocide claim, and the scaling back of the estimated Aborigine fatalities. Shameful though these killings were, the reality is that many more Aborigines succumbed to introduced diseases. Smallpox, possibly introduced by Macassan fishermen from the north, the now Indonesian island of Sulawesi, may have killed up to half the Aboriginal population in 1789. Smallpox did not come with the First Fleet. It was not recorded on the ships and in any case, a smallpox infection would not have survived the long voyage from England. Smallpox may again have killed up to half the Aboriginal population between 1824 and 1831 and a third of the population in the tropics and remote outback in the 1860s.

'History is not about the imposition of belated moral judgments, it is not a balm for hurt minds,' says Inga Clendinnen, author of *Dancing With Strangers*, the acclaimed book reconstructing the experiences on both sides for the first years after 1788.

'Clendinnen does not line up with orthodox academics who see the settlement as the beginning of 150 years of violence and the dispossession for the first Australians,' Stephen Matchett wrote in the *Australian*. 'In her telling, the better of the British officers appear to be admirable men, sensitive to the people they were dispossessing.

'But neither does she share any apparent allegiance with the triumphalists who want the modern Australian story to be a heroic achievement in which the Aborigines were collateral damage in nation building.'

Clendinnen's even-handed approach is shared by Australia's most eminent historian, Professor Geoffrey Blainey. In the 1993 John Latham Memorial Lecture, Blainey posed the question of the treatment of Aboriginals. Was it an ineradicable stain on Australian history? There are many answers, he concluded, each of them a part-answer. The lecture passed without attracting controversy or great attention, but, three years later, when John Howard used an evocative and powerful phrase from it – 'the black armband view of history' – Professor Blainey found himself at the centre of fierce debate.

Some of the points he made in that lecture include the following:

> To some extent my generation was reared on the 'three cheers' view of history. This patriotic view of our past had a long run. It saw Australian history as largely a success. While the convict era was a source of shame or unease, nearly everything that came after was believed to be pretty good. Now the very opposite is widely preached . . . a rival view, which I call the 'black armband' view of history. In recent years it has assailed the generally optimistic view of Australian history . . . [and which] . . . might well represent the swing of the pendulum from a position that had been too favourable, too self-congratulatory, to an opposite extreme that is even more unreal and decidedly jaundiced.
>
> Many Australians see the treatment of Aboriginals, since 1788, as the blot on Australian history. Fifty years ago, fewer than 50,000 Australians probably saw this as the blot. Now maybe

several million are convinced that it is the main blot and maybe half of the population, or even more, would see it as highly regrettable. Irrespective of whether deep shame or wide regret is the more appropriate response, this question will be here to vex or torment the nation for a long time to come.

My own view on this question is much influenced by my own particular interpretation of Australian history. My starting point you might disagree with, but I have held it for some 20 years, have often reconsidered it, and will hold on to it until contrary evidence arrives.

The meeting of the incoming British with the Aboriginals, at a thousand different parts of Australia spread over more than a century, was possibly a unique confrontation in recorded history. No doubt a version of the episode happened somewhere else, hundreds of years earlier, on a smaller scale. But there is probably no other historical parallel of a confrontation so strange, so puzzling to both sides, and embracing such a huge area of the world's surface. If we accept this fact we begin to understand the magnitude of the problem that appeared in 1788, puzzled Governor Arthur Phillip, a man of goodwill, and is still with us. It will probably remain with us for the foreseeable future, defying the variety of quick-fix formulas that sometimes attract the Federal Government, tempt the High Court, and tantalise thoughtful Aboriginal leaders.

In 1788, the world was becoming one world. Europe's sailing ships had entered nearly every navigable sea and strait on the globe, and the ships' crew were alert for anything that was tradable, and so they were sure to return to any place of promise. In 1788, the industrial revolution was also beginning. Here landed representatives of the nation which had just developed the steam engine, the most powerful machine the world had ever known, and also the semi-mechanised cotton mill. On the other hand Australia represented the way of life that almost certainly prevailed over the whole habitable globe some 10,000 years earlier. The Aboriginals had no domesticated plants and animals and therefore a very different attitude to the land – this is part of the long painful background to the Mabo case. They had no pottery, they had implements of wood and bone and stone but none of metals, they had no paper and no writing, though they were skilled at a variety of other signs. They had no organisation embracing more than say 3000 people and probably no organisation capable of putting more than 200 people into a battlefield at the one time. They had few, if any, permanent villages, and only a token ability to hoard food. They believed in a living, intervening god – here was a close resemblance – but not the God seen as the correct one. It was a society with many distinctive merits, often overlooked, but it was startlingly different to the one that supplanted it.

In 1788, Aboriginal Australia was a world almost as remote, as different as outer space. We now think of Aboriginal Australia as having a unity, but it had even less unity than Europe possesses today. There were countless economic and social differences, and an amazing variety of languages. Accordingly the idea, widely voiced now, that the incoming British could have – should have – signed a treaty with the Aboriginals, and so worked out rights and compensations, rests on a faith in the impossible. Any treaty would have been one-sided, with the Aboriginals as losers.

Even if the First Fleet had brought out not the dross but the wisest and most humane women and men in England, and even if the Aboriginals whom they met at Sydney Harbour were the wisest of all their people, how conceivably could a treaty have been signed – given the differences in language and understanding? And if a treaty were signed, how far inland and along the coast would it have extended? The north and south sides of Sydney Harbour, then as now, had different languages and tribal arrangements. (I do not use this argument, incidentally, to comment on the question of whether there should or should not be a treaty today.) There was a huge contrast between the two cultures, the incoming and the resident. Every Australian still inherits the difficult consequence of that contrast.

How can we fairly summarise this complex and delicate question: was the treatment of Aboriginals an ineradicable stain on Australian history? There are many answers, each of them a part answer.

Anyone who tries to range over the last 200 years of Australia's history, surveying the success and failures, and trying to understand the obstacles that stood in the way, cannot easily accept the gloomier summaries of that history. Some episodes in the past were regrettable, there were many flaws and failures, and yet on the whole it stands out as one of the world's success stories. It is ironical that many of the political and intellectual leaders of the last decade in our history are so eager to denounce earlier generations and discount their hard-won successes.

Many young Australians, irrespective of their background, are quietly proud to be Australian. We deprive them of their inheritance if we claim that they have inherited little to be proud of.

Whoever might be seen as the 'winners' in the ongoing history wars, the debate has put the treatment of the Aboriginal Australians back in focus. Today the debate is not about genocide, but dysfunctional communities, child abuse, health and education, alcohol and drugs. It is about our mutual future.